T0129190

RECIPES FROM THE
GORGE RANCH

RECIPES FROM THE
GORGE RANCH

ROBERT HOGFOSS

RECIPES FROM THE GORGE RANCH

iUniverse books may be ordered through booksellers or by contacting:

iUniverse
1663 Liberty Drive
Bloomington, IN 47403
www.iuniverse.com
1-800-Authors (1-800-288-4677)

ISBN: 978-1-5320-1075-0 (sc)
ISBN: 978-1-5320-1076-7 (e)

Library of Congress Control Number: 2016921203

Print information available on the last page.

iUniverse rev. date: 02/17/2017

Dedicated to my sons, Jess and Luke
and to
all the friends and family who have joined us at our table

Note: our property is inside the Columbia River Gorge National Scenic Area, with a quarter mile frontage on the river. A beautiful spot. This land was home to Sahaptin speaking tribes along the north bank of the Columbia (Yakama, Klickitat, etc.) for millennia. The first non-Indians to live here were a German family that came west on the Oregon Trail in the late 1800s, and established a cherry orchard, vineyard and large garden (including a large planting of asparagus). They raised cattle and sheep, but over time the ranch fell into disrepair and abandonment. In 2012 a wildfire burned all the original buildings and fencing. The spirit of the place (and the asparagus gone wild) lives on. It is probably more appropriately called 'a nice house with a big back yard' now, instead of a ranch, but we still call it that.

TABLE OF CONTENTS

SOUPS

APPETIZERS

SIDE DISHES

MAIN DISHES

DESSERTS

INTRODUCTION

Our family has a small ranch on the north bank of the Columbia River, inside the Columbia River Gorge National Scenic Area (which straddles Oregon and Washington along the Columbia River), about an hour east of Portland. Eagles, Falcons, Coyotes, Bobcats, Black Tailed Deer Meadowlarks and Quail are our neighbors. Dozens of different species of native wildflowers cover the ground each spring. It is, quite simply, a beautiful place. I love this place, and I have come to love to cook for friends and family.

Living in the Columbia River Gorge provides us with a bounty of fresh and local foods, from organic vegetables to wild game, salmon, steelhead, fresh fruit, local wines and more. There are fruit orchards, vineyards, dairies and local cheese makers close by. There is a Buddhist retreat nearby that produces multi-colored eggs from chickens who run free in an orchard at the foot of 12,000' foot Mt. Adams (thick shelled eggs with deep orange yolks). Overall, this is a good place to slow down, and a good place to cook and enjoy good food with family and friends.

This book gathers some recipes that have proved to be perennial favorites at the ranch; nothing fancy or complicated. In fact, many are prosaically basic (but good). The book was put together to respond to enquiries from family and friends for recipes they have eaten with us. The recipes are not intended to reflect any special diet or philosophy of food, but all of the recipes are based on fresh, local and organic ingredients. No matter where you live, you will do well to choose fresh, local and organic foods. It occurs to me in proofing this book that there are no beef recipes here (although you can substitute beef for bison, elk or venison in the handful of recipes that call for wild game). There are no processed or packaged food as ingredients here, either, and only a couple of references to canned goods (*e.g.*, for a non-local ingredient like coconut milk). Almost all of the recipes also happen to be very low in carbohydrates and fat. I guess that is what fresh, local and organic will do for you. You could do much worse. Americans in the 21st century are doing much worse with their diets every day, unfortunately.

All of these recipes are easy to make, and healthy for you. Most of them can be made in less than 60 minutes, many in less than 30 minutes. A few are incredibly simple and familiar, but they serve as reminders to keep things simple, and enjoy simplicity. Each recipe indicates the amount of time it takes from start to table, and states the origin of the recipe (and in some cases, origin of the dish itself). Each recipe comes with a bit of a story, which is what eating with family and friends is all about.

So, enjoy. Give these recipes a try. Then create your own new stories.

BACKGROUND

Like all families, our extended family always had a few naturally gifted cooks in the mix (those who can make anything taste wonderful, with creative instincts about using different ingredients). Those naturals at cooking got our son Jess interested, and eventually led him to culinary school in Charleston, S.C., and then work as a professional chef. After 9/11, Jess volunteered to be a Combat Medic with the Army, and went to Iraq. A major life change, to say the least. He was able to call me almost daily from Iraq, often from various outposts in active combat zones. Jess was stationed first in Tal Afar, and then Ramadi, when both of those places were some of the most dangerous locations in the world. When Jess called me, gunfire and mortars were often heard in the background, but he was always calm. I had been a backcountry medic during a decade of forest firefighting in my youth, so Jess and I would discuss medic issues. But those are sober discussions under any circumstances, much less from an active combat zone.

In an attempt to change the topic from the difficult situations Jess found himself in when he called, I asked him to give me some basic cooking instructions. I did that mostly to keep his mind off combat for a little while. True to form, Jess took my request seriously, and he began to give me detailed cooking instructions by phone, by memory and from an active combat zone on the other side of the world. Remarkably impressive, when you think about it.

I actually picked up a good bit from those phone calls, and I finally got interested in cooking. I do not have the natural instincts for cooking that we all admire, nor Jess' professional training and experience, but I do OK at the 'cook' (not chef) level of following a recipe, and I've come to enjoy it immensely.

So, this is really just a list of some of my favorite things to cook, which by definition are easy (or I could not have mastered them). The major theme is fresh, local and organic, but there are minor themes on Southern cooking, because we lived on an island off the South Carolina coast for many years, and on Norwegian related dishes, because our family is originally from Norway (the Norwegian recipes are kept to a minimum, though, because when is the last time you saw a Norwegian restaurant?) All of the recipes have been tested and adjusted based on comments from Jess, his brother Luke, and various extended family members, friends and visitors. When I started college all I knew how to do was boil water and make toast (seriously). I quickly learned, however, that even basic cooking can be easy and fun, and preparing food can be its own form of meditation. These recipes are all relatively quick, all pretty damn good and all guaranteed to impress those you are cooking for (we are all impressed by having someone else cook for us in any event). This is really just another form of essential knowledge about living in the world, about being mindful of what we choose to sustain ourselves with on a daily basis. This kind of knowledge is best when passed along from family and friends.

Jess' 'Combat Cooking' instructions began with a directive to get a copy of the large 'Culinary Institute of America' cookbook, and read it (it truly is the best cooking reference book, and you are encouraged to get a copy if your interest is strong). You don't need any book, however, to do these recipes. Next, Jess instructed me on basic knife and cutting techniques. I admit that I never really mastered that (to this day, Jess and brother Luke worry every time they see me pick up a knife to chop – so use common sense!) From there, Jess had me start with soups. I love soup, so that was fun, but Jess said you can't 'graduate' soup until you master a perfect consommé. I didn't do that, either, but even Jess acknowledges that the soups I'm passing along here are very good, and easy to do.

The most important thing Jess taught me about cooking by far (also 'the only thing I really learned'), is the French concept of *mise en place* ('everything in its place'). What that means in practice is that _before_ you start cooking, make sure that you have all the ingredients gathered and prepped (cut, chopped or measured), and all the required pots or pans and utensils at hand. If you do that, everything goes surprisingly well. If not … well, for me it's often a harried mess. I made a dinner for several friends recently that had five burners going at once, all with different ingredients, different cooking times and temperatures. Daunting, especially while trying to carry on conversation with guests. But, I had carefully prepped each dish and had all ingredients measured and lined up in order. I had my _mise en place_ working, in other words, and it all came out perfectly.

These recipes are all tried and true, and all worthy of addition to your tool kit. Enjoy: this is sustenance; this is life and the living; and above all … this is about family and friends.

Bob Hogfoss (2016)

ABBREVIATIONS AND BASIC TIPS

"C" =   1 cup (2 C to a pint; 4 C to a quart; 16 C to a gallon)

"T" =   1 tablespoon (16 T in a C)

"t" =   1 teaspoon (3 t to a T)

"lb" =   one pound by weight or volume for liquids (16 oz)

"oz" =   one ounce by volume

"a dash" is just that (intended to be subjective, but a slight amount)

"to taste" means add a small amount first, taste and then adjust

---

* Estimated cooking times are meant to include prep, so remember to do your *mise en place*

* Keep your knives sharp (electric sharpeners are surprisingly cheap, and old fashioned steel and whetstones are even more reasonable).

* Whenever possible and sensible, replace water with chicken stock (not for coffee or tea, of course … or for large pots of water, but whenever appropriate)

* Whenever possible, replace butter with olive oil in a recipe; it's healthier for you.

* Use fresh ground pepper. It's cheap, and so much better than pre-ground.

* Get good salt. Get some *fleur de sel* as one of several salts, if you can find it, or any large crystal or coarse kind of salt. It is surprising how many good salts are making it to even remote markets. We get a wonderful alder smoked salt in our local cowboy town, which is great for certain dishes.

*   *Note to the above: Americans eat way too much salt generally, but that primarily comes in prepared and processed foods. Although salt is a critical nutrient for health, and an essential ingredient to good food and taste, moderation is required. But don't worry. If you do home cooking you will find that it is almost impossible to salt the food too much … you will never add as much as you get in processed or prepared foods.*

*   Be flexible and creative! Despite the admonition to understand and rely on the concept of *mise en place*, that doesn't mean you have to be rigid. If you don't have the right ingredients, improvise. If there are ingredients you know you are not fond of, replace with something else. Experiment. You might just invent something new that is much better than the plan.

*   Finally, this is not baking, so no need to be precise with the measurements; just roll with it.

TOOLS and PREPARATION

KNIVES, POTS AND PANS

If you are going to do any cooking, you need a few good _knives_. You will need to spend at least $100 total for a few good knives (you can spend much, much more, but you will need to spend at least that). You need a 10" to 12" stainless steel knife for general work, and a smaller 4" or so paring knife. After that, branch out.

You also need to keep your knives sharp. Electric _sharpeners_ are surprisingly reasonable in price now, but you can also use a steel and whetstone. In using any knife, hold it near the bolt where handle and blade meet, with thumb and forefinger pinching the tool. Keep the knuckles of your other hand folded back as you hold the food being cut. When chopping, place the tip of the knife on the cutting board and rock the rest of the blade up and down, for best control.

You will need several _cutting boards_. Any kind will do, and you will come to have your preferences, but have at least two or three at hand. Bamboo is increasingly common, and a good choice (easy on knives, hard and antibacterial).

For _pots_, you need at least two, preferably stainless steel. One should be a large 10-12 quart pot with lid, and another smaller saucepan in the 1-2 quart range, with lid. For _pans_, you cannot beat cast iron. I use a 12" cast iron deep Dutch Oven pan almost daily, that came from my Norwegian grandmother. I also use a 6" cast iron frying pan, a cast iron casserole and a cast iron grill pan at least once every week. Keep them seasoned (sesame oil works best) and they just get better with age. Just wipe them out with hot water after use, not soap (use a little steel wool lightly to loosen any dried food), and they're good to go. Steel pans are fine, too, but avoid Teflon or coated pans, as they wear out quickly and are less responsive to heat variation than iron or steel (although I admit to keeping a 12" teflon pan for doing omelets ... it's just so easy).

Oh, and _hot pads_, obviously. And for basic utensils you need several wood or steel long spoons (at least one slotted) for mixing and serving, a whisk, a spatula, a colander and a set of measuring spoons and cups.

A couple of recipes in this book call for a food processor or simple hand mixer, but you can chop and mix on your own if you don't have one. I only rarely use a processor.

MISE EN PLACE ('MEEZ-UN-PLOS')

This concept is taught in every culinary arts school and every good kitchen worldwide. Do not be intimidated by the term, but do not ignore it. It truly is essential. It not only saves time, but it lets you concentrate on the cooking without racing around. *'Mise en place'* simply means having everything in place, <u>*before*</u> you start cooking. So <u>prep</u>: measure or pour, cut or chop all of your ingredients and put them in bowls or other containers in order of use. Then get the pots and pans and utensils you will need and set them out. If you do that, the process of cooking will be so much more enjoyable than the other option – racing around, and getting a bad result.

MIRE POIX ('MERE-PWAH')

Mire poix should be a staple for you. It is nothing more complicated that a sauté of three chopped vegetables: onion, carrot and celery, in a ratio of 2:1:1 (*i.e.,* half of much carrot and celery as there is onion). These three veggies, usually sautéed in olive oil or butter, are known as 'aromatics' in cooking terms, and they are the base of a large number of dishes, especially soups, stocks, sauces, etc. You can chop the mix rough or fine, add some herbs or not, use them raw or cooked … but they are simply a staple if you are going to be doing any cooking.

Mire poix is sometimes confused with what is often referred to as "*the Holy Trinity,*" being the equivalent of aromatics used in New Orleans cooking. The Holy Trinity simply replaces the carrots in *mire poix* with bell peppers. That's it. The Italian equivalent for an aromatic veggie mix is "*Soffritto,*" which simply adds garlic to the onion, carrot and celery mix.

So. Mystery of terms solved, right? But once you start incorporating and adjusting YOUR version of *mire poix* or its variants to your cooking, you will find it essential.

Personally, I make a *mire poix* at least weekly, often as a meal by itself. I admit, though, that I always add chopped mushrooms, and there's not even a name for that mix that I know of (other than 'good').

ROUX ('RUE')

Several of the included recipes call for a simple roux, which is nothing more than a thickener used in various soups, sauces and other dishes. The method comes from classic French cooking in the 18th century. Roux can be 'white,' 'blond,' 'dark' or 'chocolate,' with the difference being solely a result of how long you let it cook and darken. Darker roux has a more nutty taste.

The simple formula for roux is roughly equal parts (by weight) of flour and fat. The fat is usually butter, but it can also be olive oil or bacon grease (Cajun recipes often call for the latter). Making a roux is relatively easy. Making the classic French sauces (there are five) is much more of a challenge, and more the province of a true chef than cook (not required for any recipes in this book). For the recipes in this book, you can use equal T of butter or olive oil and flour (*e.g.,* 4 T melted butter with 4 T flour slowly mixed in). The trick to making a good roux is stirring continuously after you add the flour, until you get the color and consistency you want. Then you typically add chicken broth or milk and keep stirring.

SPICES

"Spices" in regard to food are generally considered to be any form of vegetable or mineral substance that adds to the taste presentation of the food stuff, often providing preservative, aromatic or pungent qualities. Humans have used spices at least since we learned to cook with fire, if only because there are certain minerals and vegetable compounds that we need to maintain health (*e.g.*, salt, iron, etc). We later learned to use certain plants to help preserve foods (*e.g.*, chili peppers). By the late 1500s, as ships began exploring the globe, we encountered new plants that offered unique preservation, flavor or visual properties for food. Those new gems were brought back to other parts of the world, and cooking – and good food – flourished.

If you enjoy cooking, you will inevitably build quite an array of spices, and some will be your perennial favorites. Essentials include: good salt and pepper; both fresh and dried thyme, rosemary and parsley; cayenne and red chili peppers; fresh cilantro; tarragon; dill; cumin, turmeric and curry; paprika (regular, smoked and spicy if you want to explore); etc.

There is an incredible history of human exploration, culture and trade surrounding spices, and each spice has a story to tell that will give you an appreciation of what we so take for granted in today's world. Do a little research on a spice you like, and you might pick up some new ideas on how to use it (and you will definitely add a story to the meal).

BE CREATIVE, BUT KEEP IT SIMPLE

As already noted, improvise if you find you don't have the right ingredients, or you would prefer some alternative ingredients. Be careful with the number of ingredients and spices used in any dish, though; you always run the risk of adding too much and getting a 'muddy' tasting result (I have done that way too many times). You will find that a simple touch is best, both with ingredients and spices.

As an example, here is an incredibly simple but always popular way to prepare chicken breasts or thighs…. drizzle with a little olive oil, sprinkle with a bit of salt and pepper, and put in oven at 375-400 degrees for about 30 minutes. The result will amaze you at how flavorful and moist it is; simple.

BREAKFAST

Breakfast Pizza
Croque Monsier/Croque Madame
Eggs any way (fried, boiled, poached, coddled)
Egg Mess (from Vienna)
Ranch Omelet
Rocky Mountain Toast
Smoked Trout (or Steelhead) and Potato Hash with Baked Eggs
Tassajara Cinnamon Rolls
Three Great Poached Egg Variations

BREAKFAST PIZZA

Serves 4-6
20 min (90' if making dough for crust – recommended)

This is hands down the best 'found' recipe I ever tried. It came from the tiny but popular 'Big Sur Bakery' in Big Sur/Yosemite, where it was long a favorite with locals. It is a surprisingly flavorful alternative to a breakfast sandwich ("life changing" said the New York Times in an August 2008 review). The only thing similar to pizza is the appearance (if you make it round), as there is no sauce, but there is a wonderful doughy flavor with otherwise familiar breakfast staples, all in a nice presentation.

Note the recipe below varies slightly from the NYT published version, tempered by years of living under the guiding light of the Tassajara Bread Book (and now scores of trials making this recipe). The recipe below is for one 16 inch round pizza (or two 12 inch), but you can make it in a baking dish as well.

Ingredients

For the Dough

Note: you can use a pre-made, uncooked pizza crust if you want, but if you do, consider sprinkling some fresh thyme or rosemary on it. Easy to make this dough, though, and you should try (it's from the Tassajara Zen Center cook book).

1 C warm water

1 pkg dry active yeast

2 T olive oil

¾ t salt

3-3.5 C flour (2 C for initial mix, plus another 1 – 1 ½ C for kneading)

Optional but recommended: add a bit (1/2 to 1 T) minced fresh thyme to the water/yeast mixture before adding any flour. It makes a piquant dough, and the crust looks nice.

For the Toppings (this is for 1 large, 16" pizza)

6 strips thick cut bacon [optional if you have veggie guests]

½ C grated parmesan cheese

2 – 3 C fine cut mozzarella cheese (1 or 2 7 oz pkg shredded)

6 large eggs

2 T minced flat leaf parsley

2 T minced chives

2 green onions, thinly sliced – or – 2 to 4 T chopped leek (white part), or 1 minced shallot

Salt and fresh ground pepper to taste

Preparation

For the Dough

1. sprinkle 1 pkg yeast on 1 C warm water and let sit for 5'
2. add 2 T oil, salt and about 1 C flour; stir for 5' with wooden spoon (this helps release the gluten and gives the dough a wonderful flavor)
3. continue to add another 1-2 C flour while stirring; when the mix doesn't stick to spoon roll out on floured surface, then knead while adding more flour as necessary
4. form a ball; place in oiled bowl; cover with a warm wet cloth and let rest at room temp for 1 hour [optional: cover and refrigerate dough overnight, then take out and let warm for an hour before continuing in the morning; more flavor to the dough]

5. punch down dough after it has risen; knead into flattened pizza round(s) or rectangles (use fists under dough to expand while turning)

Making the Breakfast Pizza

6. preheat oven to 500 degrees; set for lowest rack
7. sprinkle a little corn meal or grits on pizza pans (to prevent sticking); lay dough on pan and press to fit; pinch edges with fingers or fork and cut off any excess
8. sauté the bacon if using, then drain/dry on paper towels and tear or chop into pieces
9. sprinkle mozzarella, parmesan, bacon pieces and chopped leek or shallot on the dough
10. crack six eggs on each pizza, evenly spaced (helps to first make a little 'nest' in the cheese for each egg, to locate and contain egg placements)
11. bake on low rack for 12' to 14' (may take a few minutes more depending on oven)
12. remove from oven and sprinkle parsley, chives and more leek or shallot on the pizza
13. let cool for 2' to 5'; cut and serve

… and (breakfast) surprise; it's great!

CROQUE MONSIER/CROQUE MADAME

10 – 15 minutes; serving size for 2

Our sons Jess and Luke accompanied us to Paris several times when they were young, and they returned alone for a wonderful visit when Jess was on leave from being a Combat Medic in Iraq and Luke was still in high school. All of us simply love this breakfast sandwich you can buy on the streets or in the shops of Paris every morning. It's so different from America's ubiquitous breakfast sandwich, and it is easy to make in your own kitchen. Note that the only difference between the two versions is the addition of a fried egg to the Madame.

"Mister Crunch" is the literal translation of "Croque Monsieur" (also called a "Toastie" in Holland, England and elsewhere). Quick to make and a real treat. There are several different versions of this dish in the U.S., and more in France, but this is one we like, and it is simple to make (does not require preparing a béchamel sauce). We also prefer the open face version (perhaps showing our Scandinavian heritage and influence).

Ingredients

2 slices of bread, crusts cut off (use a nice dense bread like sourdough or potato, or just your favorite)

~2-3 T butter

~4 oz thinly sliced ham (the better the ham, the better the sandwich)

~4 oz gruyere cheese, thinly sliced (or use sliced mozzarella, swiss, etc … but gruyere best)

1 T or so of good mustard

2 eggs, fried separately (if making "Madame," which is better, I think)

Preparation

1. melt butter in a large frying pan; place bread in pan to brown slightly
2. remove bread from pan, and to _browned_ side of each slice add the following:
   a. spread some mustard on the bread
   b. place a slice or two of ham on top
   c. followed by a slice of cheese
   d. repeat the above process, ending with cheese
   e. [optional: add some grated cheese on top]
3. Meanwhile, fry the eggs in a little butter (sunny side up or over easy)
4. Put the bread slices back in your initial frying pan with a tad more butter, cover and heat until the bottom of the bread is browned and the cheese is melted
5. Place the eggs on top of the sandwiches, sprinkle with a bit of salt and pepper, and serve!

EGGS ANY WAY

There may be no better food than eggs. Natural, abundant, high in protein, and they come in their own package. There is a huge difference between organic, free range eggs and those that come from factory farms, and it's well worth choosing the healthier alternative.

Lara Ferroni in Portland has a wonderful book called <u>Put An Egg On It</u> (Sasquatch Books: 2013) that presents a number of surprisingly creative egg dishes. She also well summarizes what many cookbooks and chefs say about 'the basic rules of preparing eggs.' So, with acknowledgements to Lara and many others, but with my own edits, here is a short summary of the best way to prepare different types of egg:

<u>Boiled Eggs: Soft, Medium or Hard</u>

<u>Method 1: Steaming</u>

Bring a few inches of water to boil in a pot, with a vegetable steamer placed in the pot. Place the eggs in the steamer and cover the pot while continuing the rapid boil. *<u>5 min for soft boiled; 8 min for medium; and 12 min for hard boiled</u>*. After steaming, put the eggs in a bowl of ice water to cool, then peel.

<u>Method 2: Boiling</u>

Put eggs in a pot of cold water, with enough water to cover the eggs. Using medium heat, bring the pot to a boil, then *turn off the heat*, cover the pot and let the eggs sit to desired level of finish: again, its *<u>5 min for soft boiled; 8 min for medium; and 12 min for hard boiled</u>*.

Fried Eggs: Sunny Side Up, Over Easy or Over Hard

Put 1 – 2 T of butter or olive oil in a small pan over low heat. Once the butter is melted or oil warm, gently drop or slide the eggs into the pan. For _sunny side up_, cover the pan and let cook (over low heat) for 5 min. For _over easy/over hard_, leave the cover off the pan but prepare as you would for sunny side up, then flip the egg(s) and cook further on the other side: 20 seconds for over easy and about 2 min more for over hard.

Scrambled Eggs

Beat or whisk the eggs with an ounce or two of milk, half 'n half or cream. A little butter or oil in the pan, over medium-low heat. Stir the eggs with a spoon or fork as they heat, and continue to stir as the mix cooks. You can add cheese, cream cheese, fresh thyme, salt and pepper or other ingredients as the whites begin to harden. The slower you cook them the better the result.

Poached Eggs

My sisters and I grew up thinking that poached eggs were a special treat, because our mother just loved them. They are indeed special. On her last day in hospice, our mother awoke from a semi-coma to ask politely for a poached egg and some ice water. She enjoyed both, and then gently passed away a few hours later, children at her side. Poached eggs as a sweet last request.

So, to make poached eggs: bring about 2 inches of water in a pan to just below a simmer over medium heat (just when little bubbles begin to form on the bottom of the pan). You can drop the eggs into the water at that point, or if you want more fancy results, crack the eggs individually into a ramekin, add a drop or two of vinegar to each ramekin, and then stir the water with a whisk to create a gentle whirlpool while you slide each egg into the swirling water. The vinegar and the whirlpool help keep the egg white more contained. Our mother always spooned hot water gently over the egg yolks as they cooked, which makes a nice looking finish. Remove eggs from water with a slotted spoon. Great on English Muffins. Great any way, always.

Another way to poach eggs, especially if you are making a number of them, is to use a muffin tin. Preheat the oven to 350 degrees. Put 1 T water into each muffin tin holder, then slip an egg in, and add a dash of salt of pepper. Bake the eggs in the oven for about 13-15 minutes, then gently remove from the muffin tins.

EGG MESS (FROM VIENNA)

10 min; serving size variable

This is the first thing I learned to cook at Reed College (conveyed by a girlfriend who learned this while growing up in Vienna). Quick, good and a little bit different. I still cook this one today, and Luke in particular loves it. The first time I had it was with a group of friends, who said, 'This is fantastic; what do you call it?!' My girlfriend replied, 'Eggs.' Our friends found that unacceptable and instead proclaimed that it would henceforth be called 'Monica Mess.' She objected strongly, thus it is became named, simply, 'Egg Mess.'

Ingredients

1-2 T butter or olive oil (more if for more than 2 people)

1 medium tomato per person, diced into chunks

1 egg per person

½ C cottage cheese per person

About 1/3 C mozzarella or other shredded cheese per person

2 – 4 oz parmesan cheese as garnish (optional)

Salt and ground black pepper

optional

about ½ sliced shallot per person (or green onion equivalents)

about ¼ C sliced mushroom per person

chopped Italian/flat leaf parsley or chives as garnish)

Preparation

1. melt butter or warm oil in pan, at medium high heat

2. add tomato pieces and cook until softened (several minutes)
3. add shallots (or green onions) and/or mushrooms if desired
4. add eggs, and stir until scrambled
5. add cheese, salt and pepper and stir
6. add cottage cheese, and stir all together
7. add garnish if using

-- a surprisingly good 'egg porridge' --

RANCH OMELET

10 minutes; serving size variable

We make this often at the Ranch. Quick, amenable to various ingredients (leftovers help), looks good in presentation and somehow seems more filling than just fried or scrambled eggs. When I was in Bhutan a few years ago with my sister Carol, I found that eggs and omelet 'variations' are a staple even when the overall cuisine is very different. Eggs are always good.

Ingredients

1 egg per person

Couple ounces milk, half 'n half or cream

1 – 2 T olive oil or butter

Salt and pepper to taste

Beyond that, add filling; a few herbs and cheese is a standby, but any of the following are also great:

Cream cheese (put a few dabs here and there)

Use a different cheese as topping once folded (like Parmesan or Romano)

Mushrooms (Shitake or Chanterelles are superb, but any mushroom is good)

Diced shallots or green onions

Chopped, cooked shrimp (Balsamic Grilled Shrimp, below, are great for this)

Lox, smoked salmon or trout

Chopped parsley or cilantro

Few drops of vanilla

Preparation

1. use a large (10" to 12") skillet over medium heat
2. mix eggs with milk or cream in a bowl with a fork or whisk
3. if using mushrooms or onions/shallots, sauté them first until soft (although you can also just add them raw to the egg/milk mix, which is quicker and still works fine)
4. pour egg/milk mix into skillet and let cook for a minute or two
5. using a spatula, lift up the edges of the egg as it cooks, to let the runny parts of the mix get to the heated surface; do this several times around the pan
6. as the egg whites begin to color, add your filling ingredients
7. once the whites are cooked, add remainder of fillings, then flip one half of the omelet over the other with a large spatula; add some salt and pepper and any topping herbs, parm cheese, etc.
8. serve

-- lots of room for variations on this theme –

ROCKY MOUNTAIN TOAST (OR 'EGGS IN A BASKET')

10 min; serving size variable

This is so simple it's ridiculous, but it's the very first thing I learned to 'cook' as a first year at the University of Chicago. Still fun, especially for kids. As Amalie Little (the daughter of my dear friend and partner Catherine Little) often says: it's easy-peasy, lemon-squeezy.

Simply tear a hole in the center of a slice of bread (any kind of bread will do), then melt some butter in a frying pan at medium heat, and lay the bread in the pan; after a minute or two flip the bread over and break an egg into the hole. Add some salt and pepper, let cook until egg white starts turning opaque, then gently flip again for about a minute or less ... and serve. Easy-peasy!

SMOKED TROUT (OR STEELHEAD) AND POTATO HASH WITH BAKED EGGS

about 30 minutes; serves 4

This recipe comes from that wonderful book called <u>Put An Egg On It</u> by Portland author Lara Ferroni (Sasquatch Books: 2013). Works great with smoked trout (or smoked Steelhead, which is available in the NW and technically a trout), but also works with smoked salmon or slab bacon cut into cubes. A few adds and suggestions here, but basically Lara's recipe. Excellent treat for a slow morning with guests.

Ingredients

1 sweet onion, chopped

1-2 cloves garlic, minced

2 or 3 medium potatoes (preferably Yukon Gold), cut into ½" cubes (skin on)

~2 T olive oil

~2-4 oz smoked trout or Steelhead (or smoked salmon, cooked bacon cubes, etc.), torn into bite

size pieces

~2-4 T cream cheese (whipped preferably)

~2 T cream (optional)

~1/4 to ½ C shredded mozzarella cheese

4 fresh eggs

1 T fresh thyme

Several good dashes of paprika (smoked, preferably)

Salt and pepper to taste

Tabasco sauce (to individual taste of diners)

Preparation

1. preheat oven to 350 degrees
2. parboil potato cubes (drop in boiling water, return to simmer for about 3'-5' until just tender); drain under cold water and set aside
3. in large oven proof pan (cast iron Dutch Oven is perfect) heat olive oil and sauté onions for about 5', until tender
4. add garlic and drained potatoes to pan; sprinkle with paprika, salt and pepper, and continue cooking until potatoes start to turn golden brown (about 8' or so)
5. place cream cheese in dabs around top of potato mix, drizzle the 2 T cream over pan (if using), and sprinkle some mozzarella over all
6. arrange smoked fish around top of pan, sprinkle with more salt, pepper and paprika (and more mozzarella if you want)
7. make small indentations in each quarter of the potato mix for the eggs, then drop unbroken eggs into those nests
8. sprinkle more mozz, salt, pepper and paprika, then place pan uncovered in oven
9. let cook about 10', until egg whites are cooked but yolks are still soft
10. use a large spoon to scoop out servings of the mix with an egg on each; set out some Tabasco sauce.

TASSAJARA CINNAMON ROLLS

~1.5 hours; serves 4-6

The Tassajara Zen Center is located in the Pacific Coast mountains just inland from the Big Sur coastline, south of Carmel, California. It was the first Zen center established outside of Asia, dating to the late 1960s when Shunryu Suzuki founded it. The Zen Center is isolated (and it's a harrowing drive over steep ridges and rough gravel roads to get there), so from the beginning it has had to be self-sufficient. Thus, the Tassajara kitchen was born, and it has become legendary for incredibly good food.

The Zen Center published the "Tassajara Bread Book" in the 1970s. It is now out of print, but you can still find used copies. It was a bible of my limited cooking for many years. The process of making bread as a meditation is worth trying. I made various breads from the Tassajara Bread Book for large gatherings for many years, to warming appreciation. The Tassajara instructions for making Zen-like bread dough is used here (and for Breakfast Pizza, above). I have spent some time at the Tassajara monastery, and have spent several 'work sessions' in the fabled kitchen. Such history. Such food. These rolls are special; made carefully and eaten in happiness.

Ingredients

For the Dough

1 C warm water

1 pkg dry active yeast

2 T olive oil

¾ t salt

3-3.5 C flour (2 C for initial mix, plus another 1 – 1 ½ C for kneading)

For the Rolls/Filling

¼ C melted butter

¾ brown sugar

1 T or more of cinnamon

½ C or more of raisins [optional]

Preparation

1. sprinkle 1 pkg yeast on 1 C warm water and let sit for 5'
2. add 2 T oil, salt and about 1 C flour; stir for 5' with wooden spoon (this helps release the gluten and gives the dough a wonderful flavor)
3. continue to add another 1-2 C flour while stirring; when the mix doesn't stick to spoon roll out on floured surface, then knead while adding more flour as necessary
4. form a ball; place in oiled bowl; cover with a warm wet cloth and let rest at room temp for 1 hour [optional: cover and refrigerate dough overnight, then take out and let warm for an hour before continuing in the morning; more flavor to the dough]
5. punch down dough after it has risen; roll it out to a rectangle about ¼" to 3/8" thick
6. brush the dough with the melted butter, then sprinkle on the brown sugar, cinnamon and raisins (adjust the sugar and raisins to make a more or less sweet roll)
7. roll the dough up fairly tight, then cut into ½" to ¾" slices, and place on a greased sheet pan (allowing some space between rolls for expansion)
8. preheat oven to 375
9. let rise for 20 minutes, then brush with egg wash (simply an egg whisked with a fork and a splash – less than 1 T – of milk or water) and bake for 20 to 25 minutes

-- every meal should be a meditation –

THREE GREAT POACHED EGG VARIATIONS

As noted elsewhere, poached eggs have always been a special treat for our clan. Here are three very nice variations for serving them.

<u>ONE: Poached Eggs on Rosemary Scented Parmesan Toast</u>

10 minutes; adjust servings as desired

This is remarkably simple and quick, but a real flavor surprise.

---

1. heat 1 or 2 T olive oil in a large pan
2. rub a sprig of fresh rosemary around the pan, and let heat for a bit
3. remove the rosemary and place slices of thick bread (or half an English Muffin) in pan
4. cook at low medium heat for a minute or two, then flip the bread over
5. sprinkle about 2 T of grated parmesan cheese on top of each piece of bread; cover and let heat for a couple of minutes
6. meanwhile, make poached (or fried) eggs
7. put a piece of rosemary-parmesan bread on a plate, with the egg on top, and serve with a bit of fresh ground pepper (there's already salt in the parmesan)

-- simply amazing combination of flavors and textures –

TWO: Poached Eggs on Grits with Prosciutto or Pancetta

serves 4; 20 minutes

Yes, more poached eggs, but this is so good. Takes a bit longer than just making eggs, but worthwhile. Adjust for servings, but follow the same ratios for grits. You can change prosciutto for pancetta. A surprisingly well matched compliment to the delicacy of poached eggs.

Ingredients

1/3 C white or yellow corn grits (you can mail order the best there is from Anson Mills in Charleston, S.C.)

1 C cream

1 C whole milk

1-2 T butter

[optional, for cheesy grits: -1/2 to 1 C shredded mozzarella or cheddar cheese, to taste]

Salt and fresh ground pepper

-3 oz of prosciutto or pancetta

4 eggs

Preparation

1. bring the milk and cream to simmer in a saucepan; slowly stir in the grits and let simmer uncovered for 15 to 20 minutes, stirring often (cook long enough so grits get fairly thick)
2. heat the prosciutto or similar thin meat in a pan with a bit of olive oil until crisp, and set aside
3. a few minutes before the grits are done, in a separate pan, heat water to the point that tiny bubbles form, but before a

full simmer; crack eggs into the water carefully, and let cook uncovered for a couple of minutes until egg whites firm up

4. remove grits from heat, stir in some butter, salt and pepper; stir in shredded cheese if using
5. drain water from eggs
6. put a small ladle's worth of grits on plate, break up pancetta into pieces and place over the grits
7. add a poached egg over the grits/pancetta on each plate, and a touch of salt and pepper

*-- wonderful creamy grits mix perfectly with
the egg yolks, cheese and pancetta –*

THREE: *Grilled or Sautéed Asparagus Over Poached Eggs*

Same as either of the above, but top with some asparagus that have either been grilled (stove top cast iron grill works fine), or flash sautéed over high heat. Use olive oil in either method.

SALADS

Acorn Squash, Goat Cheese and Arugula Salad
Basic green salad
Caprisi (Tomato, Basil & Buffalo Mozzarella)
Curried Crab Salad with Watermelon and Arugula
Duck Breast Salad
Lemon Cous Cous Salad with Shrimp and Spinach
March Hare
Pacific Rim Salad
Scallops Poached in White Wine on Spinach Leaves
Tomato & Red Onion Salad
Warm Lentil Salad with Goat Cheese on Arugula
Wutermelon, Mint & Feta Salad

ACORN SQUASH, GOAT CHEESE AND ARUGULA SALAD

serves 4-6; about 60 min, but can be made ahead

The first time I had this salad I was very impressed, but all the menu suggested was "Warm Acorn Squash, Goat Cheese and Garam Marsala over Arugula," and the waiter offered no more help. But the description said almost all there was to it ... almost. So I tried to deconstruct the flavors, Googled a bit and experimented. Then I prepared it for my son Luke's band who had stopped by the ranch en route to play Portland, and they all loved it. It really is a wonderful blend of flavors, textures and temperatures. You can make the squash and dressing ahead of time, then quickly warm the squash, whisk the dressing and assemble the salad in a matter of moments. Well worth trying.

Ingredients (separated by each step)

1 acorn squash: peeled, seeded and cut into ½" to ¾" cubes

2 T olive oil

2 T maple syrup

½ t (pinch) of each: cinnamon, onion (or garlic) powder, and cumin

salt and pepper

3 T apple cider vinegar

1 T dijon mustard

1 t garam marsala

1 clove garlic, minced

salt and pepper

½ C olive oil

~5 oz arugula (1 pkg)

~2-4 oz crumbled goat cheese

Preparation

1. preheat oven to 400 degrees
2. put some parchment paper over a baking sheet, and add squash cubes
3. drizzle 2 T olive oil and 2 T maple syrup over squash; sprinkle with cinnamon, onion powder and cumin; mix squash cubes by hand; add some salt and pepper
4. put squash in oven for about 15 to 20 minutes
5. while the squash is baking, make the dressing by mixing together in a bowl the 3 T apple cider vinegar, 1 T dijon mustard, 1 t garam marsala, minced garlic and some salt and pepper
6. slowly pour in the ½ C olive oil to the dressing while stirring with a whisk; when combined, refrigerate the dressing

Assembly and Serving

Put some arugula on each serving plate, then sprinkle goat cheese over the greens. Drizzle with cold dressing, then top with warm squash cubes. Add a bit more goat cheese and salt and pepper to each plate, and serve. Can prepare ahead of time and reheat squash for serving.

-- the band loved it, so join along –

BASIC GREEN SALAD

less than 5 minutes; serving size variable

OK, so the only reason I am including this is to remind my sons, my nieces and nephews, my friends (and most of all, myself) how easy and healthy it is to include a basic green salad with almost any meal (I had a salad for breakfast just last week). There are so many subtle variations you can do with a basic green salad, and it is so incredibly quick. Just no reason <u>not</u> to do it more often than we all probably do.

The Greens

The best greens are, of course, those you grow in your own garden. You can choose your favorite greens and have them fresh throughout the summer. But grocery stores around the country have increasingly sourced a wide variety of greens, many fresh, organic and sometimes even local. Even the pre-packaged greens are usually quite fresh (just be sure to rinse them thoroughly).

Lettuce comes in so many forms: looseleaf, butterhead/Bibb, romaine, iceberg, hybrids. But then there are so many other types of greens readily available: spinach, arugula, kale, etc. My personal favorite is a 50/50 blend of baby spinach leaves and arugula, although I admit to having a crave for a good iceberg salad a few times a year. So pick and find your favorite.

The Dressing

For many years I did a weekly 300 mile commute, one way (600 miles total). I found that plain water kept me as awake as coffee (even slight dehydration makes you a bit sleepy). And I found that the best snack was just plain baby spinach leaves. A bit weird perhaps, but I loved it, and no dressing needed. But dressing is good when you sit at a table to enjoy a salad. So, dressing for plain greens?

You *can* serve a basic green salad as is: no dressing and no other ingredients. Not bad for a long distance commute snack. But usually you or your guests will want some dressing, or even a choice of dressing. You can find the expected standby versions in good quality at the grocery store, but you should at least try making your own. The most simple dressing is just some lemon juice over the greens, with a little olive oil. Surprisingly good and refreshing.

Beyond that, the standby salad dressing is oil and vinegar, or balsamic vinaigrette. Both are basics, and always popular.

Oil and Vinegar/Balsamic Vinaigrette

In cooking schools and restaurants this is usually called a *basic vinaigrette* or *basic French dressing*. Simple indeed: nothing more than a 3:1 ratio of oil to vinegar. But the key is to use really good oil and really good vinegar. My favorite is a good olive oil (*Picual, Koroneiki, Coratina, etc.*) with one of several different good vinegars (*apple cider, white wine, red wine, etc.*). Add some salt and pepper.

Balsamic vinaigrette is simply using balsamic vinegar as the vinegar portion.

You can put the oil and vinegar dressing in a blender, or whisk it in a glass bowl (or just shake it in a covered container). Or, you can simply pour the ratio directly on the salad (even though that will separate, I do it often). Once shaken, the oil/vinegar becomes an emulsion, which will separate in a while (so stir or shake again). You can add a touch of mayo or mustard to keep the colloidal suspension from separating, if you want.

There are several ingredients you can add to this basic dressing before you blend or whisk it: some minced garlic or shallot; a t or so of mayo or mustard; a t or two of crumbled bacon; a t or so of honey; etc. In other words: be creative.

The Extra Ingredients

No limit here; be creative. Lemon juice is always a good choice to homemade dressings. Sliced heart of palm or artichoke hearts are good. Crumbled bacon. Finely chopped shallots. Fresh herbs (thyme, rosemary, oregano, basil, parsley, cilantro).

-- keep it green –

CAPRISI (TOMATO. BASIL AND BUFFALO MOZZARELLA)

5 min; serving size variable

Another 'obvious' recipe, included just as a reminder of how quickly you can put together classic, good and healthy food. One of my personal favorites. A very simple salad, which is incredible if the tomatoes are fresh.

Ingredients

1 to 2 medium tomatoes per person, sliced round [or can chop for a variation]

mozzarella cheese, sliced (slightly less than amount of tomato slices) [or chop for variation]

several leaves of fresh basil

T or so of olive oil

T or so of balsamic vinegar

salt and ground pepper

Preparation

arrange on plate in overlapping slices, starting with tomato [or mixed chop]

intersperse basil leaves between slices [or chop up for mix]

drizzle olive oil and balsamic vinegar over

salt and pepper to taste

CURRIED CRAB SALAD WITH WATERMELON AND ARUGULA

20 min; makes 4-6 appetizer size salads

Picked up this recipe years ago (I believe the original is from NYC Chef Daniel Boulud). I've made it several times, and it's wonderfully light and crisp. A bit strange prep, because you're dealing with such tiny quantities to prepare the crab. Once done, though, the three parts of the salad (curried crab; watermelon pieces; arugula) can be refrigerated separately for several days, and then the salads can be assembled in a few minutes when you need them.

Ingredients

1 T olive oil

1 – 2 T finely chopped onion or shallot

2 rounded T finely chopped Granny Smith apple

½ C light mayo

1 T finely chopped cilantro

1 T finely chopped mint

pinch of Saffron threads

slight pinch Cayenne if desired

1 lb jumbo lump Crabmeat (cooked)

Several ½" slices of whole watermelon, rind removed and cut into ~2"/ side triangular pieces

Juice of ~ ½ lime

5 oz Arugula

2 T olive oil

Juice of ~ ½ lime

salt and pepper

Preparation

For the Crab

1. in a small saucepan, heat 1 T olive oil and sauté onion and apple
2. add curry and saffron (and a pinch of cayenne if you want)
3. remove from heat when onion is softened; add 1 t water and let cool
4. add onion mix to to mini food processor (or do this by hand); fold in mayo and mix
5. scrape mix into a bowl; add cilantro and mint, and pepper (no need to use salt at this point unless you want, because the crab will be salty)
6. fold crab into mix; adjust seasonings to taste

The Watermelon

1. cut into ½" pieces (triangular looks nice)
2. drizzle with lime juice and salt

The Arugula

1. toss the Arugula with 2 T olive oil and some lime juice; add salt and pepper

*-- serve cold: watermelon on top or next to arugula,
then heap crab over the watermelon —*

DUCK BREAST SALAD

15 min; serving numbers flexible

This is a wonderful salad that works well as a lunch or light dinner. We have lots of ducks in the Gorge, but you can find duck breasts (usually frozen) in most grocery stores. Use one duck breast per plate (they usually run about 6 oz. or so). My instinct is to grill whenever possible (I grill fruit routinely), but for this recipe prepare the duck in a pan on the stovetop and not the grill; you will control the dish much better, and it doesn't take long. Duck is greasy to cook over open flame because the skin has considerable fat (how else do you think these wonderful birds stay warm while they sleep on cold water?). The meat is surprisingly lean, though, and this recipe releases the fat without flames, then you discard the fat before serving. The result is a nicely crisped, lower fat skin, with a moist and relatively tender meat. Decidedly not greasy.

Ingredients

1 duck breast per serving

5 oz balsamic vinegar per 2 duck breasts

salt and pepper

Baby spinach and arugula mix for salads

Other salad components as you wish (tomatoes, shallots, heart of palm, etc.)

Preparation

1. [optional] marinate duck breasts in a small dish with balsamic vinegar (meat, not skin, side down), for an hour

2. score diagonal cuts on duck skin, about one half inch apart, to create a diamond cross hatch (cut the skin but not the meat if possible)

3. place a frying pan (non-stick works great for this) over medium to medium high heat; cook the duck breasts skin side down for about 4-5 minutes

4. remove the duck, pour off the grease and wipe the pan clean of grease with paper towels

5. return the duck to pan and heat, meat side down, and cook for another 5 minutes or so (for medium rare)

6. remove duck from pan, let cool a few minutes, then slice thinly on the diagonal

7. prepare your greens, with a little oil and vinegar over, then arrange the duck slices on top of the salad. Add a bit of salt and pepper and serve

-- you can't duck the result: tender, tasty and healthy –

LEMON COUS COUS SALAD WITH SHRIMP AND SPINACH

about 20 min; serves 4 as salad or 2 as a main dish

I do not remember where this recipe came from, but I do remember that I made it for Luke as our first meal when we moved back to our Gorge cabin. This is a remarkably quick and refreshing salad. You should try it.

Ingredients

1 C cous cous, uncooked (regular or pearl)

1 ¼ to 1 ½ C water

1 t lemon zest

¼ C fresh lemon juice

3 T chopped tarragon (or dill)

2 – 4 T extra virgin olive oil

1 lb large shrimp, cooked, shelled and cooled

3 C baby spinach

4 radishes, thinly sliced

8 oz Shitake mushrooms, stemmed and chopped

1 T pine nuts, dry roasted on stove top

Salt and fresh ground pepper

Preparation

1. bring water to boil and add cous cous (maybe add a bit of olive oil or butter); reduce to simmer, cover and cook for about 15 min

2. while cous cous is cooking, peel shrimp and put in pot of water just at a boil for about 3 mins; drain and reserve

3. in a large bowl, whisk the lemon zest with the lemon juice and tarragon or other herbs, then whisk in the olive oil

4. add the cooked cous cous to the lemon and herb dressing, then the shrimp, baby spinach, sliced radishes, mushrooms and pine nuts; toss to coat

5. season w/salt and pepper and serve.

-- a light and refreshing salad, for lunch or dinner --

MARCH HARE SALAD

20 min; serves 4 easy

I think this recipe came from the "Moosewood" cookbook back in the 1980s. It's been in my pile of good things to make for a long time. This was my favorite recipe while working as a forest firefighter (for those dorky 'potluck' dinners at remote ranger stations); easy to make and very healthy (kept those firefighters going)!

Ingredients and Preparation

finely chop (to about 1/8" cut) the following:

- about ½ C carrots
- about ½ C celery
- about ½ C apple
- about ¼ C leek or gr onion

add about 1 to 1 ½ C chopped tomatoes (cut not as small as veggies)

add about ½+ C chopped parsley

add about 2 C alfalfa or other sprouts

mix in 1 Quart non-fat cottage cheese

toss ingredients

drizzle with juice of ½ to 1 lemon, and about 1 T of olive oil; some ground pepper

adjust ingredients and spices to your preference

-- a very healthy and filling salad --

PACIFIC RIM SALAD

10 minutes; serves 4

This is my little riff on the cucumber salad you often get in sushi restaurants. It's light and refreshing. Quick to make. If you want a truly traditional sushi restaurant salad, just use the cucumbers and leave out shallot and tomato. Either way, try it.

Ingredients

2-3 cucumbers (Japanese or English cukes work best, but regular OK too), thinly sliced

2-4 medium tomatoes (fresher the better); seeded and cut to about a ½" chop

2 shallots; thinly sliced

2 T sesame oil

2 T rice vinegar

2 t or so of soy sauce or Tamari (dark soy sauce)

Toasted sesame seeds

Salt and pepper

Preparation

1. place the thinly sliced cucumber pieces on several paper towels and sprinkle with salt; after a few minutes put another paper towel on top and press out moisture
2. combine cucumbers, tomatoes and shallot in a bowl
3. mix sesame oil, rice vinegar and soy or tamari in small bowl; then drizzle over salad
4. grind pepper and sprinkle salt over bowl; sprinkle toasted sesame seeds on top

SCALLOPS POACHED IN WHITE WINE ON SPINACH LEAVES

10 min; by serving size

This is my own simple creation. Simple, but incredibly tasty. Guaranteed to 'wow.' Also works as an appetizer or even as a light main dish.

Ingredients

3 – 5 sea scallops per serving for salad (5 – 7 if a main course)

(fresh frozen seafood is now common, and good quality, if you need)

2 C white wine (or just enough to slightly cover scallops in the pan)

2 bay leaves

Baby spinach leaves (1 bag if using store bought)

Balsamic vinegar to drizzle

Few oz of shredded parmesan cheese

Black ground pepper

Preparation

1. Bring wine to low simmer in a pan
2. Add bay leaves
3. Add scallops, and simmer/poach for about 3 – 5 minutes (spooning wine over the tops if not covered by the liquid)
4. Put spinach in bowls, add poached scallops
5. Sprinkle with parmesan and ground black pepper
6. Drizzle some balsamic vinegar over each bowl

TOMATO & RED ONION SALAD

10 min; serves 2

Another simple salad idea. This one is completely different, though; spicy and chewy.

Ingredients

Feta cheese, crumbled (about 1 C)

2 large tomatoes, quartered, seeded at least slightly (meaning push the mushy part out) and cut into ½ in. pieces

1 medium red onion, finely chopped

1 jalapeno pepper, seeded and thinly sliced

2 T Italian (also called flat leaf) parsley, minced

3 T olive oil

Salt and pepper to taste

Simple portion ratio for ingredients:

-- use about twice as much tomato as red onion

-- use a little less feta cheese than red onion

-- adjust to taste

Preparation

1. Toss the feta with the tomatoes, onion, jalapeno and parsley
2. Drizzle olive oil over the salad, season with salt & pepper
3. toss until coated

-- serve right away or chill first –

WARM LENTIL SALAD WITH GOAT CHEESE ON ARUGULA

20- 30 minutes
serves 4 (small plates)

Lentils are simply remarkable. They entered our food chain in the Neolithic period, one of the first crops ever cultivated by humans. Lens culinaris is a legume that grows as a short (16") annual bush. The lentils appear as seeds on small pods. DNA studies show that lentils were first domesticated for food as long as 13,000 years before present, first in the Near and Middle East. Hieroglyphs in the tombs of Ramses III and at Thebes show servants preparing lentils. The ancient Greeks and Romans wrote of lentils: Aristophanes said "who dare insult lentil soup, sweetest of delicacies!" and Pliny passed down details on how to grow lentils and make soup. Hippocrates prescribed lentils to cure liver ailments. Lentils are even mentioned in the Old Testament, where Esau, starving, offered to give up his birthright title to Jacob in exchange for a bowl of cooked lentils (Genesis 25:34).

About 30% of the total calories in lentils come from protein (one of the highest protein content of any bean or nut). In addition, lentils have a very low amount (5%) of "readily available starch" (RDS), with most of the carbohydrate in the bean being "slowly digested starch" (SDS) (up to 30%). In short, a very healthy food for those with diabetes, having little (and delayed) impact on carbohydrate sugar uptake. Lentils are also a great source of iron, fiber, folate and vitamin B.

There are several different kinds of lentil on the market today. The most common is the brown lentil, but then there is the "French" or green lentil, and the wonderful "Black Beluga" lentil. The latter is very small and looks much like caviar. It cooks more quickly and has a more nutty flavor than red or green lentils.

This recipe can be made with any type of lentil, but it is especially good with the black beluga. It is meant to be a small side salad or appetizer, served on individual plates (not a large bowl). Lots of room for creativity if you want to add other garnish to the salad. The result is an attractive, healthy salad, and goat cheese compliments lentils so very well.

TIP: when cooking any lentils for presentation as a salad, use a 3:1 ratio of water or stock to beans (4:1 for soup base), and bring the liquid to boil before adding the beans. Return to a boil, then reduce heat, cover and simmer. About 30 minutes for the larger red lentils, and about 20 minutes for (French) green and a bit less (15-20 mins) for (Beluga) black lentils. In all instances, lentils are best al dente, with a bit of crunch left (not moosh).

Ingredients

3 C chicken stock or water

1 C lentils, rinsed and sorted (stones removed, if any)

1 medium shallot, diced

1 bay leaf

3 T good olive oil

1 T lemon juice

1 oz vinegar (white wine, rice, red wine) or cooking sherry

2 t brown (or cane) sugar

minced chives or flat leaf parsley (or both) for garnish

1 t coarse salt

1-2 cloves garlic, minced

[optional] 2 T capers

2-4 oz crumbled goat cheese

Salt and pepper to taste

~2 C arugula

[optional, for garnish] 1 small to medium tomato, seeded and small chop

Preparation

1. bring water (or chicken broth) to boil, and add lentils
2. return to boil then reduce heat to simmer for 5 minutes
3. add shallots and bay leaf, cover and continue simmer (25' for red, 15'–20' for green and ~10-15 minutes for black lentils … all until al dente)
4. while lentils are cooking, mix olive oil, lemon juice, vinegar, sugar, parsley, garlic and capers [if using] and salt and pepper
5. strain lentils (use fine strainer for Black Beluga lentils); discard bay leaf
6. mix liquid with strained lentils
7. if using red or green lentils, you can add the goat cheese to the mix now, and return to heat briefly to melt and mix; if using black lentils, reserve goat cheese for use as central garnish
8. put arugula on plates or in bowls, and spoon lentil mix over
9. add goat cheese to top of lentils on each plate or bowl, then sprinkle with chives
10. add chopped tomato around plate/bowl if using; can also add a little grated Romano or parmesan cheese to the top of each serving if desired

-- enjoy 13,000 years of flavor and history --

WATERMELON, MINT & FETA SALAD

10 min; serving size adjustable

Easy as can be. A great, simple summer salad. Simple is best, but I offer a little twist that makes it even better. Try it.

Ingredients and Preparation

Watermelon cut to small bite cubes

Fresh mint, shredded

Feta cheese, crumbled

Dash of salt

Thin shavings of fresh ginger (use a potato peeler lightly)

Mix ingredients; chill; serve – with or without the salt and ginger. Either way, simple is best on this one – a very refreshing little summer salad.

SOUPS

*also works as a main dish

*Asparagus Soup with Lemon and Parmesan
Avgolemeno (Greek Lemon & Chicken Soup)
*Chicken Broth and Chicken Soup
Cold Chick Pea and Tahini Soup
*Coq Au Vin
*Corn and Bacon Chowder
Fisherman's Stew
*French Lentil Soup
Greek Salad Cold Tomato Soup
*Northwest Seafood chowder
Oyster Stew
Seafood Bisque
*Soupe a l'Oignon (French Onion Soup)
Wild Mushrooms in a Sherry Shallot Broth

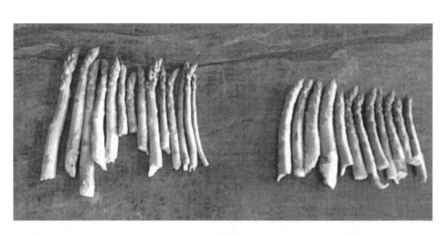

ASPARAGUS SOUP WITH LEMON AND PARMESAN

30-45 min; serves 4-6

Our family is fortunate to have some heritage wild asparagus on the ranch. The first non-Indian people to live on this property was a Dutch family who came out on the Oregon Trail in the late 1800s. They established a small homestead with a vineyard, a cherry orchard, and a big garden with a large planting of asparagus. The homestead was slowly abandoned over the next century, and then the remnants of the house and barns, vineyard and orchard all burned in a large wildfire that ran through here in 2002. But somewhere along that timeline the asparagus went feral and lives on. We look forward to its appearance every mid-to late-March, at scattered locations around the ranch (it's appearance now runs with the wind, as seeds spread), and then we eat it every day through April. We have so much asparagus over that month and a half that we are always looking for new recipes.

This is our absolute favorite asparagus soup recipe. Original came from Jenn Segal, who has a food website called "Once Upon a Chef" (www. onceuponachef.com) and describes herself as a "classically trained chef; busy Mom" (Jenn has wonderful recipes on her website, so you should check it out). Tinkered with the recipe a bit, but it gets rave reviews from anyone who tastes it. Note there is no cream, half 'n half or milk in this ... just some vegetable or chicken stock. Few ingredients, perfectly matched. The dill and thyme are critical to the result (we've experimented with using wild desert parsley (Lomatium grayii) instead of the dill, which is more sharply pungent and good, but that's admittedly hard to find except out here at the edge of the high desert plateau.

We use a chinois (<shen-wah>) – which is a large funnel shaped strainer with very fine mesh, that comes with a large wooden pestle – to strain the solids out of the soup after running it through the blender. This produces a wonderful broth like soup. If you don't have a chinois, you can use a plain large strainer to get almost the same result, or you can just serve the soup as is after doing the puree in the blender, which will be more like a split pea soup; not broth-like. Any way you make it, this is just a superbly delicate soup. Note: if you do strain the soup, you can take the solids from straining and add some back to the stock to thicken part of the soup if you want, or you can make a separate soup with the solids by adding a bit of stock and more spices … great by itself.

Ingredients

2-3 bunches of asparagus (in grocery store form), or about 2+ lbs

Cut tips off asparagus and reserve; then chop stems into ½" pieces (don't use the white/woody bottoms of stalks); should make about 4 C of stem pieces, but don't worry if the amount differs)

3 T butter

2 medium sweet or yellow onions, chopped

3 cloves garlic, chopped

6 C vegetable (or chicken) stock

¼ C Parmesan-Reggiano cheese, grated (not shredded) (another ¼ C for serving)

Juice of 1 lemon

Salt and ground pepper to taste

A bit of fresh thyme leaves and fresh dill for serving/garnish

[optional: several shakes red pepper flakes]

[optional: several T sour cream for serving/garnish]

Preparation

1. sauté chopped onion and garlic in the butter, in a large pot, until soft (~7-10 min)
2. add the chopped asparagus stems, and add broth, then bring to boil
3. reduce heat, add some salt and pepper; cover and simmer for ~30 min
4. meanwhile, boil or steam the asparagus tips for just a minute or two, then plunge into a bowl of ice water (this is optional, but it preserves the color and crispness; you can run them under cold water as an alternative); put on towels to dry
5. remove soup from heat, and working in batches, use a blender to puree the soup
6. strain the pureed soup through a Chinois or large strainer (or not; soup will be more broth like if strained) and return to pot
7. add the lemon juice, ¼ C Parmesan cheese and some red pepper flakes [optional]; adjust salt and pepper to taste
8. serve in bowls, sprinkling some more Parmesan and red pepper flakes on top, then add a dollop of sour cream to each bowl, and finish with some fresh thyme and dill leaves
9. add some asparagus tips to each bowl as a final touch

   -- truly the best asparagus soup you will ever find –

AVGOLEMENO (TRADITIONAL GREEK LEMON CHICKEN SOUP)

60 – 70 min; serves 4-6

This is a classic Greek lemon chicken soup (pronounced <av-go-LAY-ma-no>) that I figured out how to make after having it several times in the superb 'MetroFresh' restaurant in Atlanta, with my dear friend and law partner Catherine Little. The name of the dish simply means 'egg and lemon' in Greek. Sparse ingredients and simple prep; you poach some chicken with a quartered onion and carrot, remove the veggies and add a little orzo, then chop and return the poached chicken and blend in some eggs and lemon juice and parsley. It looks and tastes creamy, but there is no milk, cream or butter in it, just the magic of some egg and lemon. Vary the ratio of broth to orzo to make it either more thin or more thick. A healthy and good 'go to' soup for when you want to feel more healthy. My son Luke swears by this as a cold remedy.

Ingredients

2 T olive oil

~3/4 to 1 lb chicken breasts or thighs; skin on for rich broth (it comes off before you're done) or skin off for lower cal (I use skinless thighs for this)

6 to 7 C chicken broth

1 onion, peeled and quartered

1 carrot, quartered

2 bay leaves

¼ - 1/3 C orzo

2 eggs

juice of 2 large (or 3 medium) lemons

2 T chopped Italian flat parsley

salt and ground pepper to taste

Preparation

1. In a dutch oven or large pot, heat the olive oil and brown the chicken lightly at medium high heat for about 5-7 min, turning once
2. add chicken broth, onion, carrot and bay leaf and bring to boil, then reduce to simmer, cover and poach chicken for 30 min
3. remove chicken to cool, and spoon or pluck out with tongs the onion, carrot and bay leaf, and discard
4. return broth to boil, add orzo, reduce to simmer, cover and cook for another 20 min
5. meanwhile, remove the skin from chicken (if not skinless) and shred or cut the chicken into bite size pieces
6. beat eggs, then add lemon juice to the eggs while stirring
7. slowly add 1 C of the broth (from the pot on stove) to the egg/juice mixture while stirring, then add another C
8. remove the soup from heat; add the chicken and then slowly stir in the egg/juice mix
9. add parsley; salt and pepper to taste; serve with thin slice of lemon on top

   -- wonderfully light tasting and refreshing soup –

CHICKEN BROTH AND CHICKEN SOUP

about 60 min for either broth or soup; serves at least 6

Chicken soup can indeed cure what ails you. I look forward to roasting or grilling a chicken as much for the carcass to use in making broth or soup, as for the bird itself. You really should make broth and/or chicken soup every time you cook a chicken. Homemade chicken broth is so much more healthy and flavorful than store bought, and you can use it for many things, not just as a base for chicken soup (homemade chicken broth will transform any rice you make).

Chicken Broth

Before you make chicken soup you need chicken broth. You can use store bought, but homemade is so much better. Homemade chicken broth is also a great lunch by itself. Healthy and tasty.

-- Bring about 6 C water or store bought chicken broth (or a mix of both) to a low boil

-- add chicken carcass, large bones and giblets if included

-- reduce to a simmer

-- add salt and pepper, dried parsley, sage, rosemary and thyme

-- let simmer, loosely covered, for at least an hour (two is better)

-- use tongs or slotted spoon to remove carcass, bones and cartilage

-- remove scraps of chicken meat from the carcass and bones, and set aside for use in chicken soup or other dishes

-- adjust salt and pepper (and other herbs and spices to your preference)

--let cool and refrigerate the broth for other uses, *or* proceed to chicken soup!

Chicken Soup

1. Put one quart chicken stock (store bought or home-made) and about two cups water into a large pot and bring to a boil, then reduce to a simmer and add salt, pepper, dried thyme, rosemary and a dash of cayenne or other pepper (chili flakes, cajun seasoning, etc.)

2. Meanwhile, prepare separately ~1 C cooked (not raw) rice (Jasmine, Bhutanese Red, Wild, etc.) and let rice cool while the soup is being prepared (for the rice use ~1/3 C dry rice and ~1/2 C water or stock). Alternatively, skip the rice and put ½ to 1 C orzo or small spiral pasta directly in the soup pot when you add the mire poix, at steps 4-5 below

3. Also prepare separately (while broth is heating) a mire poix (preferably with mushrooms) in a pan (2 T olive oil; add 1 sweet onion, chopped, then half that amount of chopped celery and carrot, and ~8 oz. chopped mushrooms)

4. Add the mire poix mix and cooked rice or raw pasta (if using) to the soup pot

5. Add some chicken pieces (from the bird if you made your own broth)

6. Adjust ingredients and spices to taste, and continue to simmer for about 20'

*-- tastes absolutely great and keeps well; also good
with a dollop of sour cream on each bowl --*

COLD CHICK PEA AND TAHINI SOUP

10 minutes; serves 4

This comes from Mark Bittman, the former Food Editor for the New York Times. Mark is a wonderful cook and food activist, and he only suggests fantastic and healthy recipes for readers to try. But when I looked at this one, I thought, 'this is just watered down hummus served in a bowl!' I was completely wrong; this is an incredible soup, quick and healthy.

I must also admit that until recently I never realized that chick peas and garbanzo beans are the same thing. Sigh. Several embarrassing trips to stores looking for chick peas when garbanzo beans sat in my pantry.

Ingredients

For Soup

3 C cooked chick peas/garbanzo beans (2 15 oz cans garbanzo beans, drained)

2-3 T Tahini

Juice of 1 lemon

1 T olive oil (plus more for drizzling when serving)

1 or 2 cloves garlic, minced or crushed with husk removed

¼ t or more cumin

Salt and fresh ground pepper

~ 1 to 1½ C water

For Garnish

1 C chopped tomatoes

1 C chopped cucumber

¼ C chopped red onion

¼ C chopped pitted olives (black or green)

¼ C chopped fresh parsley (and maybe a bit of chopped cilantro)

~ ½ C crumbled feta or goat cheese

Cumin for garnish

Olive oil for drizzling

Salt and fresh ground pepper

Preparation

1. For the soup, combine all ingredients in a blender and mix thoroughly; add more water for a more thin soup (should be thin enough to pour, but not so much to separate).
2. Combine the garnish ingredients in a bowl and mix.
3. Serve immediately, or refrigerate. Scoop garnish on top of each bowl, add feta or goat cheese, a bit more cumin, then drizzle with some olive oil in each bowl.

COQ AU VIN

45 – 60 min; serves 6

Coq au vin ('coke-ah-vahn') is a classic French country recipe. Everyone in the countryside has a chicken in the yard and a bottle of wine to spare, and that is almost all you need to make this delicious and healthy stew. I have been making coq au vin since my later college days, and my current version is pretty darn good. Someone showed me how to cook this version of the recipe many years ago, and I have adjusted it over time. You will notice that coq au vin appears differently in various restaurants, so pay attention and adjust your own variation to what you like best. Try this recipe, though. It only takes 1 hour from start to finish, and your diners will be very pleased. Serve with crusty French bread for dipping. One of my absolute favorites.

Ingredients

1 whole chicken, cut up into 6 pieces (2 leg/thighs, 2 wings, 2 breasts) (buy it already cut up, or

buy it whole and cut up yourself; save the carcass for broth/soup)

4-6 slices thick bacon, cut into ¾" pieces

8 oz shitake mushrooms, stemmed and sliced into ¾" pieces

2 to 3 medium sized potatoes (I use Yukon Gold), cubed to bite size

2-3 carrots, chopped to small bite size

½ to 1 sweet onion, chopped

2 cloves garlic, diced

12 or so pearl onions, peeled

1 bottle red wine (the better the wine, the better the stew)

chicken broth to cover (about 1 or 2 cups)

6 to 9 peppercorns

2 T olive oil

2 T butter

~ 1 C flour (for coating chicken)

several dashes cayenne pepper (to your taste)

fresh rosemary, thyme and basil

salt and ground pepper to taste

Preparation

1. heat olive oil in dutch oven or deep pot; add bacon, mushrooms, onion and garlic; cook about 7-10 minutes (until ingredients well softened)
2. remove bacon mix and set aside
3. drench chicken parts in a mix of flour and cayenne (I'm fairly liberal with the cayenne)
4. add butter to the same pot you cooked the bacon mix in, and fry chicken until lightly browned (about 5' to 6' per side); add chicken parts to pan while cooking
5. meanwhile, boil potatoes and carrots in a separate pot, until just slightly tender; drain and set aside
6. add bottle of wine to chicken in the pot, then add back in the bacon mix; add pearl onions
7. add peppercorns and spices; add broth as necessary to almost cover chicken
8. cook at simmer w/loose cover for about 15' to 30'
9. remove chicken, let cool a bit, then de-bone and return all chicken parts and bits to pot
10. add potatoes and carrots to pot with chicken
11. heat through and then serve (if there are any leftovers, it gets better overnight)

-- rooster with wine, tastes just fine; coq au vin c'est bon –

CORN & BACON CHOWDER

45 – 60 min
Serves 4 as a main course, or more as an appetizer
(NB: I double the recipe every time I make this, because it's that popular)

Still on soups. This one is simply incredible – not low calorie, but guaranteed to impress your diners (this is one of those dishes to use if you really want to 'wow' but have little time or practice). Thomas Keller created the "French Laundry" restaurant in California, which is widely considered to have been one of the best restaurants in the country for many years. His original Executive Chef was Jonathon Benno, and I found this recipe years ago in a zine article/interview with Benno (no longer remember the source). It is superb. I have made it many times, always to great acclaim. It only takes about 1 hour start to finish. As always, it helps if you have your mise en place together, as Jess has instructed me time and time again, before you start (arranging all ingredients and equipment in order, before you begin).

Ingredients

6 medium ears of corn, kernels cut off (put the cobs upright on a baking sheet, then use a sharp knife to slice off the kernels); collect the kernels, then break each remaining cob in two

2 C whole milk

1 ¼ C heavy cream

2 ½ T butter

4-6 slices thick smoked bacon, cut into ½ inch pieces

2 celery ribs, finely diced

1 medium onion (Vidalia or sweet onion the best), finely diced

1 T chopped tarragon

salt and fresh ground pepper

small pinch saffron (not critical, but nice if you have it)

Preparation

1. Cover the corncobs in a large pot or pan with the milk and cream, and bring to a low simmer over moderate heat. Remove from the heat, cover, and let stand for 10 minutes, then discard the corn cobs (this releases some wonderful corn flavor from the cobs).

2. Meanwhile, in a large pan, melt 2 T butter and add ½ of the corn kernels. Cook over moderate heat, stirring occasionally, until just tender – about 10 minutes. Working in batches, add the kernels to the milk/cream mixture in a blender, and puree until smooth.

3. Melt the remaining ½ T butter in the pan you just used; add the bacon and cook over moderate heat until lightly browned – about 5 minutes. Add the diced celery and onion, and the remaining ½ of the corn kernels. Cover partially and cook until tender – about 10 minutes.

4. Add the corn kernel/bacon/onion and celery sauté to the corn puree and mix together over low heat. Add the tarragon, salt and pepper (and saffron if you have it), and serve.

-- if there's any left, it keeps well in the refrigerator –

FISHERMAN'S STEW

25 min (but only 10' active); serves 4

This is one of those recipes where the sum of the parts is completely different than the individual ingredients. Surprisingly good. Need to find fennel bulbs, but most good grocers have them. Adapted from "Real Simple" magazine (April 2009): simple indeed, and quick and healthy. Extremely good.

Ingredients

1 to 2 T olive oil

2 medium to large leeks, white and light green portions; halve and cut into ¼" slices

2 cloves garlic, sliced

1 small bulb of fennel, quartered and sliced

½ C dry sherry

1 28 oz can of diced tomatoes, including all liquid

¼ to ½ t red pepper (chili) flakes

1 lb chilean sea bass (or other white fish); skin removed and cut into 1 or 2 inch pieces

½ lb mussels, rinsed and scrubbed

1 C flat leaf parsley, roughly chopped

salt and pepper to taste

Preparation

1. heat olive oil in large pan over medium heat (Dutch oven works well)
2. add leeks and stir until just softened, maybe 2 to 3 minutes

3. add garlic and fennel and stir another 1 to 2 minutes
4. add sherry, tomatoes with juices, chili, salt and pepper; bring to boil, then reduce to simmer uncovered for about 15 minutes
5. add fish and mussels and simmer gently until fish is cooked and mussels have opened, about 5 minutes
6. stir in parsley; adjust salt and pepper if necessary

-- *serve in bowls with French bread for dipping; well worth trying* —

FRENCH LENTIL SOUP

90 min (but only 20 active); serve 4-6

Lentils are an ancient food (see recipe for "Warm Lentil Salad" in above section for history), and there is nothing like a hearty lentil soup on a cold winter day (but I also serve this soup cold on a hot summer day, and it's fantastic). Can't remember where I got this recipe, but I use it a lot, and it is both easy and great tasting. The list of ingredients looks daunting, but it's not; it is simply what makes a hearty soup (interesting side note: lentils release their carbs slowly, and the average person burns them as they're released, which means this is actually a very diet friendly option). With vegetable instead of chicken broth, this is a great vegetarian dish. The recipe below calls for some lamb, bacon or sausage, but that is completely optional... Note this is really more of a stew than soup, but you can control by adding or limiting the amount of stock.

Ingredients

~3 T olive oil

Mire poix

~2 C chopped onion

~1 C chopped celery

~1 C chopped carrot

2-3 garlic cloves, minced

6 to 8 C low sodium chicken (or vegetable) broth (homemade broth best)

1½ to 2 C lentils, rinsed and drained (green, black or mixed lentils) (I do a mix)

1 14.5 oz can of diced tomatoes in juice

2 large or 4 sm/med whole tomato, diced

-- or – 4 to 5 whole tomatoes diced if not using canned tomato

[optional: 4-6 grilled lamb chops, cut into pieces, or 4+ strips low fat bacon or sausage links, chopped (maple breakfast sausage works)]

2 bay leaves

dried thyme and rosemary

sea salt and ground pepper

good dash or two of cumin and cayenne (or chili pepper)

balsamic vinegar to taste

juice from a lemon

handful flat parsley or celery leaves, and fresh thyme, chopped for garnish

[optional: serve with fat free sour cream, Greek yogurt or cottage cheese]

Preparation

1. heat olive oil in large pot or dutch oven at medium to high heat
2. add garlic and veggies (a mire poix) and sauté until begins to brown, about 15'
3. add fresh tomatoes, lentils, stir; add canned tomatoes/juice and stock
4. bring to a boil; reduce heat
5. add spices, cover and simmer about 35'
6. while soup is simmering, grill lamb, or sauté bacon/sausage and cut into ½" pieces
7. add bacon/sausage/lamb [if using] and spices
8. add a good splash of balsamic vinegar
9. add more stock if you want to thin the soup (it will be quite thick, which is intended)
10. let simmer uncovered ~10' to 15'; add lemon; adjust spices
11. garnish parsley, fresh thyme and/or celery leaves; serve as is or with a dollop of yogurt, sour cream or cottage cheese

-- wonderfully hearty and healthy soup --

GREEK SALAD COLD TOMATO SOUP

~30 min; serves 4

This unusual dish is really a soup __and__ salad. Cold tomato soup combined with Greek Salad, in perfect balance. A lunch by itself, or a nice beginning to a light summer dinner. This recipe is adapted from the concept by Momofuku chef David Chan. Definitely try this.

Ingredients

5 large tomatoes (or equivalent if smaller size); roughly chopped

1 or 2 large shallots, peeled and thinly sliced

~ 20 or so thin slices of cucumber

¾ C sliced black olives (or 2.25 oz can)

½ C feta cheese, crumbled

2 heaping T oregano leaves

3 T red wine vinegar

1 T sherry

1-2 T honey (few seconds in microwave to liquify)

2 T olive oil

Salt and pepper

Preparation

1. in a medium saucepan, heat the olive oil and add shallots, oregano and olives.
2. cook until shallots are soft (about 5-7 min); remove from heat and add vinegar and sherry and salt; let cool.
3. pour ½ T or so of honey over cucumber in a bowl and add salt

4. in a blender, puree the chopped tomato with remaining honey and salt and pepper
5. pour the tomato puree into bowls (or serve in one large bowl); add sliced cucumbers, then shallot/olive/oregano mix; add the feta and drizzle a little olive oil and salt and pepper over

   -- delicious when served fresh; gets even better when chilled –

NORTHWEST SEAFOOD CHOWDER

~30-45 min
(makes about 6 cups or 4 bowls)

One of my all-time favorite restaurants is Jake's Crawfish in Portland, Oregon, which has been in business at the same location (SW 12th and Stark) for more than 100 years. Jake's brings in fresh NW seafood all day long, and the menu changes over the course of a day to match the fresh catch. It is a very unassuming place, with old wooden booths and an active (Irish) bar that opens into the dining area. There's a booth just to the right of the door when you enter that has a small photo of Humphrey Bogart over it (and no other notation), because Bogey used to travel up to Portland from L.A. on the train or plane many decades ago, just to eat at Jakes (and he would always sit in that booth). That kind of place.

My sons and sisters and sisters-in-law and brothers-in-law and nephews and nieces, and my dear friends and partners Catherine, Larry and Annie, have all been to Jake's with me, many times. So my favorite meal at Jake's – which would easily be my last meal if I had any say in the matter – is a mixed dozen of the freshest NW oysters available that day on the half shell, with a bowl of Jake's Northwest Seafood Chowder, which has local salmon, Dungeness crab and local wild mushrooms. Add a glass or two of the house Pinot Noir from Oregon's Willamette Valley. Heaven.

I have been trying to re-create Jake's Northwest Chowder for a while, and I think this recipe is pretty damn close. Absolutely try the original if you get a chance, but also try this. Quick to make and truly delicious (and note: I do not usually use cream here, but it still tastes rich).

Ingredients

11-16 oz Dungeness (or other) crab, shredded

8 oz fresh Salmon, cut into bite size chunks (size to eating preference)

~8 oz wild mushrooms (stemmed and sliced to bite size if too large. Shitake is perfect, but any fresh will do)

~1/2 to 1 C cubed potatoes (I use Yukon Gold) (cube size to eating preference)

1 medium sweet onion (Walla Walla, Vidalia or Mayan), chopped small

4–6 C milk, Half 'n Half or cream (vary amount depending on consistency you prefer. I have   used fat free milk and it still tastes just fine, but I'm sure Jake's uses cream)

~2 to 4 T butter (or olive oil, but butter best in this dish)

~2 to 4 T flour

fresh ground pepper and salt to taste (fleur de sec ideally, but any will do)

small amount fresh thyme and dried parsley flakes

~4 oz cooking Sherry (critical)

Preparation

1. boil potato cubes while doing next two steps (boil until firm when tested with fork); drain off water and set aside
   a. optional but very good: sauté potato cubes in a bit of butter over medium high heat until slightly browned
2. sauté onion and mushrooms in 1 to 2 T butter for about 5-8' (using a deep skillet)
3. add another 1-2 T butter in center of pot with onion and mushrooms and slowly stir in flour; continue stirring to make a roux
4. slowly add milk or cream while stirring to thicken the roux
5. add crab and salmon pieces and continue stirring
6. add potato cubes to pot

7. add spices, herbs and Sherry
8. reduce to simmer and partially cover; cook for at least 15'
9. ready to eat as is, or can be re-heated

... Heaven

OYSTER STEW

about 20 mins; serves 4

For many people, oyster stew is associated with Thanksgiving or Christmas. Not so for us. It's just a good soup for a cold day, whatever season that may occur (although you obviously need oysters to be in season). Surprisingly quick to make. Historically, you had to live near the coast (and good oysters) for this soup to even be an option, but today you can find oysters in almost all grocery stores. This recipe is an amalgam of lots of input over the years. All good.

Ingredients

About 2 pints of shucked oysters, with liquor

~1/2 C minced celery

~3 T minced shallots

3-4 C milk, half 'n half or mix of the two

~4 T butter

Salt and pepper

Several good dashes of cayenne or red pepper

Chopped green onion, parsley, cilantro and/or chives for garnish; plus hot sauce

Preparation

1. drain liquor from oysters and set aside
2. put butter in large pan at medium high heat, and add celery, shallots and oysters
3. cook veggies and oysters just until the edges of the oysters begin to curl

4. meanwhile, add milk mixture and oyster liquor to a pan over medium heat (do not boil)
5. when oysters have curled in the veggie mix, add them to the milk/liquor liquids pan
6. add salt and pepper and cook for a few minutes more, but not to boil
7. remove from heat, add cayenne, red pepper or hot sauce, and serve in bowls with garnish

--the world <u>can</u> be your oyster –

SEAFOOD BISQUE

about 45-60 mins; serves 6

Bisque is a traditional French soup (it originated in the Bay of Biscay), made from shellfish not quite ready for market (cracked shells, etc.). It is a rich broth made from sautéing or roasting the shells of crustaceans (shrimp, crab, lobster or crayfish), then blended with some pureed veggies and a little cream, and seasoned. Classically, it was often (not always) thickened with a little rice, but more recently you find bisques thickened with flour and butter (in a roux).

This recipe uses neither rice nor flour, but presents a wonderfully flavorful dish. You can add a few T of rice to the mix (wild rice an interesting twist to consider), or a dollop of rice in each bowl at service, but it's not necessary. Rice is preferable to flour if you want to maintain a more traditional and clear result. The protein is mainly shrimp, but it's even better if you add of bit of crab and make it a true 'seafood' bisque. This was a 'found' recipe that Jess and I adjusted over many trials. A bit rich (butter, and some cream or Half 'n Half if you choose to add that), but well worth your consideration (and extremely tasty). Great with a light salad.

Ingredients

1 ½ to 2 pound medium or large uncooked shrimp (16-20 count/lb size is good), shelled, with shells reserved

8 oz lump crab (optional as garnish)

6 C hot water (or replace in whole or part with chicken or vegetable stock)

~6 T unsalted butter

~2 T olive oil

2 T brandy

¾ C cooking sherry

3-5 thyme sprigs

2 bay leaves

1 medium onion, chopped

1 leek, chopped (white and light green parts only)

2 celery ribs, chopped

2 carrots, chopped

2 garlic cloves, minced

2-4 heaping T cooked rice (wild rice or Bhutanese red rice best) (optional)

2 T tomato paste

pinch cayenne

couple dashes smoked paprika (optional)

juice of 1 lemon

several T minced chives

salt and pepper to taste

Preparation

Get the broth going, then start the shrimp/mire poix.

For the Broth (made from the shrimp shells)

1. in a large pot over high heat, cook the shrimp *shells* in 1-2 T butter and a bit of salt, stirring frequently until lightly browned (~3 min)
2. add the 2 T brandy and bring to boil until most liquid is evaporated
3. add 6 C water (or stock); add a bay leaf and several sprigs of thyme, some salt and pepper

4. bring the stock back to a simmer and cook uncovered for about 20 min
5. drain the stock through a strainer or colander over a large bowl, pressing on the shrimp shells to get every bit of flavor goodness into the broth
6. discard the shrimp shell solids, and pour the broth into the pan with the mire poix and shrimp that you already have going (see below)

For the Shrimp/Mire Poix

1. while the shrimp stock is simmering, put 1-2 T butter in a large pan (Dutch oven works great) and sauté the shelled *shrimp* until red (about 3 mins); remove the shrimp to a bowl, using a slotted spoon to keep juices in pan, and set aside
2. reserve about 12 to 18 of the shrimp (the rest will be pureed with the mire poix and stock); set aside
3. using the same pan, add another 1-2 T butter and ~2 T olive oil and sauté the mire poix (chopped onion/leek, celery and carrot; add minced garlic)
4. when the mire poix is cooked to soft (~8 mins), stir in the 2 T tomato paste, cayenne, paprika and a bit of salt and pepper; stir
5. add the shrimp *broth* (from above steps), to the pan you just sautéed the shrimp in, and bring the broth back to a simmer
6. adjust spices, then add the ¾ C sherry and remove from heat again
7. working in several batches, puree the mire poix/stock/shrimp mix until smooth; setting the pureed portions in a pot while you work (then pour entire puree mix back into the large pan)
8. bring the pureed mix to a low simmer to keep warm while finishing the presentation
9. chop the reserve shrimp into pieces (your preference: bite size or minced), saving at least one whole shrimp per bowl (so 6 of them)

10. add lemon juice to the pureed mix
11. add the cut up pieces of shrimp, stir a bit and remove pan from heat

SERVICE: you can mix the chopped shrimp [and some crab if using] into the pan, stir and serve, OR pour the pureed soup into bowls, using the reserved shrimp and crab as a garnish (and either add the chives to the pot or use as garnish on each bowl)

-- seems complicated but it's not, and it's extremely good –

SOUPE A L'OIGNON

Classic French Onion Soup
~75 minutes (only 15 active); serves 4-6

There is a little café at the downstream end of the Ile St. Louis in Paris (a fabled little island in the middle of the river Seine) that serves the best French Onion Soup I ever had. This recipe (from years of trial and error) comes close, and it is truly easy to make. Requires only a few ingredients, but you should use Gruyere and Asiago cheese (substitutes do not work as well). This version is not tart like too many American attempts, and it does not slather cheese over the sides of the bowl like so many U.S. restaurants do ... the better way is to keep it in the bowl, and in proportion. Better result, better taste.

Like many dishes that are today considered treats or delicacies, French onion soup was originally a poor person's food. Onions grow in almost any soil, and with a slice of crusty bread and a little cheese and wine you can create a rich soup. The soup is also surprisingly low cal: a bowl of this soup has less than 300 calories.

Ingredients

4 T butter

4 large sweet onions; peel the onions, cut in half stem to root, then slice thin crosswise

1-2 cloves garlic, minced

~1/4 t salt to pot at start

4 ½ C chicken broth

2 ½ C beef broth

herb bundle

tie together with twine several sprigs of flat parsley, fresh thyme, and 2 bay leaves

¾ to 1 C red wine (Merlot or Cab is good, but any is fine)

1 t Worcestershire sauce

2-3 drops of Fish Sauce [optional, but some 'umami' always helps]

1 T balsamic vinegar

6-12 1" (more or less) thick slices French bread (fresh or dried; number of slices depends on size of bread & bowl)

~10 to 16 oz Gruyere cheese, sliced (make about 1/8" or so thick, OK to use several narrow slices)

several T grated Asiago cheese per bowl

salt and pepper to taste

Preparation

1. melt the 4 T butter in a large pot; add the ¼ t salt
2. add the onions and garlic, and cook uncovered over medium high heat for 35 to 45 minutes, stirring often [note: the pot will look like a big pile of raw onions for 10 minutes or so, but eventually it will all cook down and then caramelize into a wonderful soupy sauce]
3. add the broth, wine, herb bundle, Worcestershire (and fish sauce if using) and stir; bring to a simmer and cook uncovered for about 20 minutes, then remove herb bundle
4. add the 1 T of balsamic vinegar, some salt and pepper to taste (not too much salt; there is salt in the cheese), then turn off heat and cover to keep warm
5. put the bread slices on a pan under a low to medium broiler to toast [if your broiler does not have temp settings, just set the pan at least 4"-5" inches below the broiler]; turn the bread once – only takes about 30 to 90 seconds per side to toast; remove pan but keep broiler on

6. ladle onion broth into large oven proof bowls, to ~3/4 full, then place one or two pieces of toasted bread in each bowl (depends on size of bread and bowl)
7. add sliced pieces of Gruyere to cover each piece of toast, with a little over the soup as well, then grate Asiago over each bowl; add a bit of salt and pepper to each bowl
8. place the bowls on the pan you used to toast the bread; place under broiler for a few minutes, until the cheese is melted and bubbly, then remove and serve

-- absolutely tremendous soup; leftovers great, too --

WILD MUSHROOMS IN A SHERRY SHALLOT BROTH

20-30 minutes; serves 4

Surprisingly complex flavors in a very easy and quick soup; perfect for spring or fall, but any time is good. A 'delicate yet earthy' soup (says the original recipe that I saw somewhere many years ago; there are several versions still on the net). This is a quick and easy recipe to remember: it only has 4 ingredients, all of which involve the number "1": 1 C diced shallot; 1 lb chopped mushrooms; 1 C dry sherry; and 1 quart chicken broth. The soup/ broth tastes slightly different every time, even if you use the same type of mushrooms, because mushrooms have such variability in flavor. One of my absolute favorites. Works great as an appetizer or a light lunch/dinner with a small salad (excellent with Pacific Rim Salad).

Ingredients

1 lb mixed mushrooms of 3 or 4 different types (stems removed from shitake and button;

bottoms of stems cut off from others), sliced to various size [my favorite mix is chanterelles, oyster, enoki and shitake, but crimini or portobello or button work fine]

1 C chopped shallots

1 to 2 T butter (just enough to saute the shallots and shrooms)

1 C dry sherry

1 quart (4 C) chicken (or vegetable) broth

fresh thyme (8 to 12 sprigs' worth)

salt and ground pepper to taste

Preparation

1. saute shallots in butter until lightly browned (about 4')
2. add mushrooms and some thyme
3. continue cooking until mushrooms are lightly browned (about 5' to 8')
4. add sherry and bring to a boil, stirring
5. add broth, cover and return to boil; simmer about 2' to 3'
6. season with salt and pepper

-- serve in bowls with thyme sprigs; superb --

APPETIZERS

*(*also work as a Side or Main Dish)*

*Ahi tuna (Tuna Tartar or Tuna Tataki)
*Balsamic Grilled Shrimp
Cheese, Glorious Cheese
Chilled Asparagus in Red Wine Vinegar
Cured Salmon with Cracklings, Roe and Yogurt Mint Sauce
Olives and Olive Oil
Panko Tomatoes
Pickled Asparagus
Sabal Trail Biscuits
Shrimp Two Ways: Poached and Pickled
Viking Wrap Variations

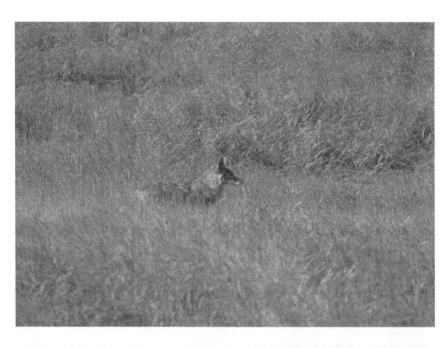

AHI TUNA (TUNA TARTAR OR TUNA TAKAKI)

about 10 minutes; serving size variable

You can find sushi grade tuna in many places in America today (we find it in the small but hip town of Hood River, Oregon near us). Be mindful of concerns about maintaining a sustainable tuna fishery, and ask about that before buying. But when you can get some high quality tuna, here are two recipes that are simply delicious. Both of these recipes are very quick and easy to make (easy peasy Japanesey, as my dear friend and law partner Annie Cook says…and her brother is a full time expat in Japan, so she should know!)

Ingredients

For Either Tuna Tartar or Tuna Tataki

~4-6 oz fresh tuna per person

Several T good soy sauce per serving size

Several T good rice wine vinegar per serving

~1-2 T sesame oil per serving

Dash good salt and pepper

For Tuna Tartar Only

~¼ to ½ diced avocado per serving size

~1 to 2 T minced shallot per serving size

~½ T roast pine nuts or sesame seeds per serving size

~¼ C small chop small cucumber (English best) per serving size

~3 T finely chopped green onions per serving size

~1 T lemon juice per serving size

Small dabs wasabi or horseradish if available

Preparation

Tuna Tataki

1. marinate tuna steaks for at least 5 mins in vinegar, soy sauce and sesame oil, with salt and pepper
2. grill tuna on hot grill (375-400 degrees) for only about 30 to 60 seconds per side (just enough to get a good sear)
3. let cool a bit and slice on the bias, then serve

Tuna Tartar

1. chop tuna into about 1/8" to ¼" pieces
2. marinate tuna pieces in large bowl with vinegar, soy sauce and oil
3. add other ingredients and gently toss
4. drain tuna mix with slotted spoon as you place into wineglasses for service, *or* pack tuna into a large round glass to the top, for later serving inverted on a plate
5. in either case, chill in the fridge for at least 15 mins, or longer
6. invert the tuna if in a glass onto a plate and remove glass (or serve as is in wineglasses)

BALSAMIC GRILLED SHRIMP

about 10 – 15 min; serves 6 or more

Something we just started making in our outdoor 'River Room' along the Intracoastal Waterway on an island we lived on for years near Beaufort, S.C. Perfect marinade combination, and a perennial favorite as appetizer or side. The grilled shrimp has a smoky, natural taste, and guests enjoy peeling the shells (which come off very easily after grilling). Note that the marinade is the opposite of a traditional vinaigrette; more vinegar than oil. Measurements of marinade not critical.

Ingredients

2 lbs large shrimp (16-20 count per pound is good)

shells off or on (we used butterflied shrimp with shells on when we lived on the island, which you can do simply by making a cut on the back of the shell to fold it flat or nearly flat, which allows the marinade to soak in more and the shrimp to swell on the grill, for better flavor);

but plain is just fine; but leave the shells on, to hold the marinade while cooking

about 1/8 to ¼ cup oil (sesame, canola or olive)

about ½ to 1 cup balsamic vinegar

juice from 1 or 2 lemons

fresh ground pepper and ground sea salt

Preparation

1. mix the marinade in a large bowl or deep baking dish
2. toss the shrimp with the marinade and let sit for at least 10 to 15 minutes
3. season w/salt and pepper;

4. cook over a medium high heat grill (about 350 degrees) for ~1-2 minutes on each side
5. remove from grill, let cool a bit and serve in a clean bowl (with a second bowl for shells)
6. tastes great hot or cold

-- a truly popular appetizer; always good --

CHEESE, GLORIOUS CHEESE

This is just an unabashed "homage to fromage." Cheese in all its forms is a blessing to us all (well, except those who are seriously lactose intolerant or have diets that omit this essential life ingredient). Most of us do eat cheese, though, and it is used in almost all forms of cooking. Cheese typically has almost no carbohydrates, but it is rich in nutrients: calcium, vitamins A and B12, etc. It is also high in protein per ounce. Since it is made from milk, it does contain fat, but that varies by the type of cheese (hard cheese has less fat than soft).

Cheese is one of our oldest foods. The best guess is that it was discovered when early humans carried milk in the stomachs of slaughtered animals. The natural rennet enzymes in the gut turned the milk to curds (probably similar to our current cottage cheese). But by 2,000 years ago, cheese making had evolved and was being written about by the Greeks and Romans.

There are hundreds of kinds of cheese. The most basic distinctions are, first: 'hard' or 'soft,' and then; 'source' (whether the milk is from cow, sheep, goat, water buffalo, etc.) Interestingly, it's not just making the cheese that affects how good it will be, it's the aging and 'refining' (or 'ripening') of it. There is a wonderful job called an "Affineur" (or Affineuse), originating in France. The term literally means 'refining,' but it encompasses the tasks of picking good cheese from a producer, then aging, turning and generally caring for that cheese until it is precisely ready for market. It may mean very carefully monitoring temperature during the ripening of the cheese, wiping off moisture from some types of cheese, spraying mist on others or rubbing aromatics into the rind. Some of the more famous modern affineurs are Herve Mons and Marie-Anne Cantin (try anything you see from these wizards). In good cheese shops – and they are growing in the U.S. – look for those names, or ask the cheese monger about affineurs and recommendations.

If you love cheese, one of the best things is to visit a "fromagerie" in Paris or other cities that appreciate this food stuff, where the cheese is laid out in baskets without wrapping or packaging, and you can pick it up and smell it (if you are bothered by that lack of packaging you are not a true cheese aficionado!) Many good American food stores will give you tastes of any cheese.

What follows is a short list of a few basic cheeses that should be in your repertoire, and a note on what they are typically best used for. All of these cheeses make for wonderful appetizers. You can prepare a cheese plate with other items (such as grapes, nuts, olives, etc.), and display a mixture or themes of different kinds of cheese as either an appetizer or a dessert.

The Basics

Mozzarella: you may be surprised, but this is the most popular cheese in the U.S. as of this writing (likely because of our mass pizza consumption). Made from water buffalo milk; white in color; originated in Italy. A semi-soft cheese with a neutral but flavorful taste; melts well in any dish. Typically served fresh or not long after, so little to no aging.

Cheddar: a hard cheese made from cow's milk, usually orange or off white in color, originated in England (but no national standards of type or quality). Typically aged for a year, more or less. Everyone loves a good cheddar cheese, but if you look you will find an incredible variety within this basic category: mild, medium, sharp, smoked, etc. It works well as a snack, as the base for sandwiches, on pasta, etc.

Parmesan: a hard, crumbly cheese made from cow's milk (fed with grass); typically white or off white in color; originated in Italy (and often called "Parmigiano-Reggiano"); used most often as grated cheese in cooking. Distinct saltiness in flavor, from brining done as part of processing; usually aged up to 12 months.

Swiss Cheese: a generic name given to a wide variety of medium hard cheeses made from cow's milk. Originated in Switzerland, but the more authentic version is true Emmental. Decomposition of the lactic acid in milk produces carbon dioxide which 'bubbles' and forms the holes or 'eyes' in Swiss cheese. Used in sandwiches, eggs and for other toppings. (A personal favorite is 'Norway Swiss,' or Jarlsberg, which has a nutty flavor).

Other Favorites

Asiago: Originated in Switzerland, a semi-hard cheese made from cow's milk, yellow in color. A fruity and buttery cheese. Excellent as an appetizer, but especially good in specific dishes (as noted in this book).

Blue Cheese: another broad category (including Roquefort, Gorgonzola, Maytag and Stilton); characterized by the introduction of penicillin spores and molds, which create blue streaks (the cheese is pierced during aging to allow more air in to support the mold; hence the blue streaks). Strong, musky flavors. Used primarily as an addition to salads or dishes in small amounts, crumbled or melted (but good as an appetizer, too).

Brie: a soft cheese originating in France, made from cow's milk. Typically more subtle than Camembert, largely because of added cream (higher milk fat than Camembert). Excellent as appetizer, with fruit or as spread. Typically served with little to no aging.

Cambozola: a relatively recent addition to the world of cheese (20th century); a combination of camembert and blue cheese (Gorgonzola), both using penicillin for flavoring and striping; less strong that most Blues; used primarily as an appetizer.

Camembert: a soft, spreadable, rich cheese made from cow's milk, originated in France. White to yellow in color, typically aged six to eight weeks. The rind consists of a fungus comprised of penicillin; taste more earthy than brie. Quality varies widely, but good camembert is exquisite. Usually eaten as is, or as an appetizer.

Chevre: semi-soft cheese made from goat's milk, white in color. Sharp flavors that vary greatly by the diet of the goats. Produced fresh (no aging). Excellent when crumbled in salads or over pasta, or as blended into other dishes.

Feta: a soft, crumbly white cheese, originated in Greece. Made from goat or sheep milk. Salty and moist (brined in salt in production). Little aging. Used crumbled in salads or other dishes.

Gouda: a semi-hard to hard cheese, white to yellow in color. Originated in Holland. Aged between 4 weeks and 12 months. Served as appetizers, grated, or melted in various dishes.

Gruyere: a hard yellow cheese, made from cow's milk. Originated in Switzerland. Salty, nutty and buttery. Excellent in various baked dishes, and pairs well with Asiago (perfect for French Onion Soup). Typically aged for 3 to 10 months.

-- all hail the cheese mongers! --

CHILLED ASPARAGUS IN RED WINE VINEGAR

~10 min (plus an hour or more for chilling; serving size variable

There are so many variations on this theme, but the idea is simply this: steam some thin asparagus, then marinate them with some vinegar, shallots, garlic and spices, and let them chill. Makes great appetizers.

Ingredients

1 to 2 lb fresh asparagus, thin as possible (pencil thin is perfect)

1 shallot, minced

1 to 2 cloves garlic, minced

½ to 1 C red wine vinegar

Some smoked (or regular) paprika

Salt and fresh ground pepper

[optional: fresh chopped or torn tarragon, or fresh thyme leaves]

Preparation

1. find the natural break in an asparagus stalk, and cut the rest to match
2. immerse asparagus into a pot of boiling water for just a few minutes (until tender but still a bit crispy), then remove and put immediately into a large bowl filled with ice water
3. remove the asparagus once cooled and dry on paper towels
4. put asparagus into a small serving dish and pour over vinegar
5. add herbs and spices, and refrigerate for an hour

CURED SALMON WITH CRACKLINGS, ROE AND YOGURT MINT SAUCE

about 45 min; serves 4

This is from Seattle chef Tom Douglas. Quick to make and a most unusual appetizer or first course. You will need to find or order two unusual spices (Togarashi and Aleppo Pepper), but it's worth it. Togarashi is a chili pepper from the genus <u>Capsicum</u> (as are most of our peppers). It usually comes as a blend of several different varieties of chili and other ingredients (as in 'Saschimi' togarashi). It's a common table condiment in Japan, used on eggs, soba noodles, ramen, fish, soups, rice, etc. Aleppo pepper is also from the <u>Capsicum</u> genus, but in this case originally from Turkey. It is named after the Syrian city so ruined by recent conflict. It was a common trade good on the Silk Road for centuries. You really don't need both, but if you can get just one go for the Togarashi. Or use a dash of cayenne instead.

Ingredients

¾ pound center-cut skin-on salmon fillet

¾ cup sugar

3 tablespoons Aleppo pepper

½ cup kosher salt, plus more for seasoning

Togarashi, for sprinkling

½ cup whole-milk yogurt

¼ cup chopped mint

salmon roe, for serving

Preparation

1. Using a sharp knife, carefully remove the salmon skin from the fillet and reserve. Thinly slice the salmon across the grain a into ¼ inch thick pieces.
2. In a medium bowl, whisk the sugar with the Aleppo pepper and the ½ cup of kosher salt.
3. Line a large rimmed baking sheet with parchment paper. Spread half of the sugar mixture on the parchment paper and arrange the salmon slices on top. Sprinkle the remaining sugar mixture evenly over the salmon and refrigerate until the fish is slightly firm, about 30 minutes.
4. Meanwhile, preheat the oven to 325°. Spread the salmon skin on another baking sheet lined with parchment paper, silvery side up, and sprinkle with Togarashi. Cover with another sheet of parchment paper and another baking sheet to keep the skin flat.
5. Bake the skin for 30 minutes, or until crisp. Remove the top baking sheet and parchment paper and let the skin cracklings cool, then break into pieces.
6. Fill a large bowl with cold water. Rinse the cured salmon in the water, rubbing off the sugar mixture. Transfer the salmon to paper towels to drain, and pat thoroughly dry.
7. In a small bowl, whisk the yogurt with the mint and season with salt. Arrange the salmon slices on plates or on a platter and garnish with the cracklings and roe. Serve with the mint yogurt.

-- the salmon can be prepared through Step 4 and refrigerated overnight --

OLIVES & OLIVE OIL

Like the above entry regarding cheese, this is an unabashed recognition of how incredible olives and olive oil are in the tool kit of any cook. Several years ago we tried to plant an olive grove for producing olive oil on the ranch. Did lots of research and talked to lots of folks, all of whom suggested that we were probably too far north to make it work. Olive trees are generally intolerant of winter temperatures that fall much below 15 or 20 degrees F for any length of time. We planted 40 plus trees in a test plot, of a dozen varieties (note to the Gorge Commission if reading this: it was part of our garden, exempt from permitting, OK?). We kept close notes on which variety did best. To our pleasant surprise, we had a respectable crop of wonderful olives. My good friend Larry Bracken flew out from the East Coast to help harvest the tiny produce (remarkably generous volunteer migrant labor by a nationally prominent lawyer.) But alas, the following winter we had temperatures fall below zero for several days, which is unusual here, but not rare. Thus ended our olive grove experiment.

But you can find excellent olives and olive oil with increasing frequency throughout the U.S. There is a great book, well worth reading, called Extra Virginity, by Tom Mueller (W.W. Norton & Company, 2013), that well chronicles the history and intrigue associated with olives and olive oil. Olive trees, Olea europaea, are native to Asia Minor, but first flourished in ancient Greece and the Mediterranean. Olive trees are among the oldest trees cultivated by humans. Archaeological evidence shows that olives were being used to make olive oil as long ago as 6000 B.C. Today's modern cultivars for olive trees all descend from those wild strains.

Greek mythology said that the Goddess Athena gave the first olive tree to Zeus as a gift, which he treasured for the many uses of olives and olive oil: light, heat, food, shade, medicine and perfume. Over time, olive branches became associated with skill in athletics or wisdom ('laurels') and with peace (the offering of an 'olive branch').

Olives themselves require some form of curing to be palatable (you cannot eat the hard little olives right off the tree). The curing process is relatively easy, though; you can do it as a home project if you get raw olives.

Most olive oil today is produced in Spain, followed by Italy, Greece and other countries (but Spain produces more than twice as much as any other country). On the other hand, per capita annual consumption of olive oil is currently highest in Greece, followed by Italy and Spain (more than twice as much consumed in Greece per capita than either Italy or Spain). In the U.S., an increasing number of olives are being produced, and an increasing number of olives used for oil are being produced here. Always look for 'extra virgin' olive oil, but do a little research on what you buy. Use a restaurant grade olive oil for cooking (heat drives off the flavors from the more artisanal oils). But search for, or order, good artisanal olive oils. Use them unheated on salads, pasta, almost any dish after cooking but before serving (including fish, poultry and meat). It always enhances the flavors and it is _good_ for you.

Get a mix of cured olives for use on appetizer plates. One of my favorites for that is the Castelventrano olive, which is wonderfully buttery in flavor. And get several artisanal oils. My favorites include Leccino, Picual and Koroneiki. It's good for you!

PANKO TOMATOES

20 min (only 5 active); serves 4

Incredibly easy, but a completely different way to do tomatoes for appetizer or salad. There are lots of recipes for Panko stuffed or baked tomatoes, but I can't remember where I found the idea to simply serve Panko encrusted tomatoes raw. It may have born of necessity (in a crunch for time), but you and your diners will be pleased.

Ingredients

4 medium tomatoes, fresh as can be

2-4 T olive oil

6-8 oz Panko bread crumbs (found at any grocery)

About 4 oz shredded Parmsan cheese

Salt and fresh pepper

Dried thyme and/or rosemary (optional)

Preparation

1. Slice tomatoes to ½" and lay on baking sheet
2. Drizzle with olive oil and sprinkle with salt
3. Let sit (it technically 'macerates' instead of marinates) for about 10 min; then turn over and repeat
4. Put Panko (Japanese) breadcrumbs on a large plate; add shredded parmesan cheese, salt and pepper and any other spices you want (or you can get Panko with spices)
5. Press the Panko onto the tomato slices on both sides, shake free any loose crumbs and then serve on plates.

-- a simple taste treat that is proportional to the freshness of the tomatoes —

PICKLED ASPARAGUS

about 60 minutes; quantities variable

I know, I know...there are already just too many references to asparagus in this little book. But we have this wonderful source of heritage wild asparagus here, and you can get fresh asparagus almost year around in good grocery stores, and these pickled asparagi are just such perfect little appetizers to go with a good beer or glass of wine on an afternoon, or on any table at lunch or dinner.

Asparagus officinalis has been used as a consumable vegetable by humans for at least the past 5,000 years (as reflected on the walls of some Egyptian tombs). The first known written recipe book in the world (Apicius' book from the third century A.D. in Rome) included reference to asparagus. The plant is native to Europe, but now grown around the world. It appears to have come to the U.S. in the mid-1800s (and came to our ranch via the Oregon Trail only shortly thereafter).

"White" asparagus is especially popular in Germany and northern Europe, but it is the same plant, created simply by piling dirt around the emerging shoots to keep them from activating photosynthesis. It is a perennial plant, but if you do not pick (snap) the shoots when young they will quickly begin to seed, after which the stalks are too woody to eat. Asparagus typically produces for about 4 to 6 weeks a year, which varies by location. At our ranch, it appears from about mid-March through April. In much of Europe, it is thought of as an April arrival, sometimes lasting to early June. Commercial production of asparagus is now common throughout the world (China is a large producer), and it can be grown almost year round.

This is a very healthy vegetable. No fat, low sodium, rich in vitamins and minerals. And yes, it does make your urine smell unique, for a little while. But well worth it!

__Ingredients__ (this makes about 4-6 one pint jars of canned and pickled asparagus)

about 3 lbs/bunches of asparagus, rinsed

4 C water

4 C white vinegar (at least 5% acid)

6 T pickling salt (or any salt will do)

3 T sugar

10-20 black peppercorns

½ to 1 t of each: pickling spices; cumin seed; allspice; celery seed (others you like, such as dill etc.)

1-2 lemons, sliced in round pieces about 1/8" thick

red pepper flakes for sprinkling in each jar before canning

Preparation

1. Sterilize your jars and lids by boiling for several minutes, or running through the dishwasher; time it so you are ready to can when they're still warm and clean
2. Hold an asparagus up against one of your jars to measure where you will cut; make sure the cut vegetables will leave a good inch between their tips and the underside of the lid
3. Cut all of the asparagus to that length and set aside
4. Combine water, vinegar, salt and sugar in a pot and bring to a boil, stirring to dissolve the salt
5. Reduce to a simmer, add peppercorns and spices, and let cook for about 10 minutes
6. While the pickling solution is simmering, fill a large soup or canning pot with hot water, and put on stove under high heat
7. Put a round slice of lemon into the bottom of each canning jar, then fill each canning jar with as many asparagus as will fit

8. Ladle the pickling solution into each jar until it just covers the asparagus (should still be some air space between the liquid and the bottom of the jar lid)
9. Put the lids on each jar and tighten finger tight
10. Gently drop each jar into the pot on stove with heating water; add water if necessary to cover the jars by an inch or two
11. Bring water with jars to a boil, and maintain a gently rolling boil for 10 minutes, then turn off heat and let jars cool in pot for another 10 minutes
12. Remove jars from canning pot with tongs and hot pads, wipe off and set aside
13. The lids should 'pop' sealed within a few hours; if any lid has not, and can still be pressed down after 24 hours, then open jar and use (will keep in fridge)

Set the canned jars in a shady, cool place for about 4 weeks to pickle (you can eat them after 24 hours, but they take about a month to fully pickle). They should keep at least a year, but put in fridge after opening.

SABAL TRAIL BISCUITS

(aka 'Duchess' cookies -- but not remotely sweet)
~50 mins (only 10 active); makes ~ 40 little biscuits

Some time ago I came across several variations for "Cheese Sables with Rosemary Salt," which sounded good, so I made a batch. They were tremendous, and easy to make. Then I did some research and learned that true Sable cookies originated in France in the 1600s, and chefs over the centuries have made countless variations on them (adding almond, or lemon or other ingredients). Little discs of goodness.

But this recipe only calls for flour, grated cheese and some butter; no sugar or egg. True Sable cookies have sugar and egg. So, these are not true Sable (whether you call them cookies or biscuits). And they're not shortbread, either, because that calls for even more sugar, more butter and egg.

What these flat little discs are is a wonderful small appetizer biscuit that is sugar free, and only about 20 calories each. They are a bit crispy on the outside, and a bit soft inside. They have only a hint of cheese flavor, but that and a little rosemary and salt makes them simply delicious. They keep well in the fridge for several days.

Given the fact that these not true Sable cookies, I decided to call them "Sabal Trail Biscuits," because they are great on hikes. For reasons known only to my dear law colleagues, I dedicate this recipe to Clare Ellis!

Ingredients

½ C self- rising flour (regular flour OK, too, but self-rising a bit softer inside)

½ C grated parmesan cheese

1/3 C shredded cheddar cheese

Dash of cayenne pepper (just a dash)

7 T unsalted butter, in T slices, room temperature (15-20 seconds in a microwave works as 'room temp')

1 T minced fresh rosemary

~1/2 t salt

Preparation

1. Combine flour, 2 cheeses and butter in blender, pulsing just enough until dough comes together (it should have a crumbly appearance – not fully mixed to a ball)
2. On a lightly floured surface, make two logs from the dough, about 1½" thick
3. Wrap each log in saran wrap and put them fridge for 30 minutes
4. Meanwhile, preheat oven to 350 degrees
5. Mix the minced rosemary and salt together (press with mortar if you have it)
6. Remove dough from fridge and cut into ~1/8" discs
7. Put parchment paper on one large or two medium baking sheet pans; arrange dough discs on pans
8. Cook in bottom third of oven for ~12-15 minutes, turning front to back mid-way through
9. Remove from oven and sprinkle with rosemary salt, then let cool
10. Put discs in fridge with plastic wrap; keeps for days

-- hit the trail with treats! –

SHRIMP TWO WAYS: POACHED AND PICKLED

Two different recipes for some special shrimp appetizers. Try them both.

One: Poached Shrimp

10 minutes; serves 4 to 6

It takes very little heat to cook shrimp, three minutes in boiling water is a standard often stated in cook books. But shrimp can get tough quickly, and if you cook it more lightly it retains a surprising tenderness.

So this is simple: a 'poached' shrimp that is really just a very light immersion in boiled water, then quickly chilled in ice water. Serve with some lemon and good olive oil or truffle oil, then a little salt or truffle salt if you have it (you don't want to use both truffle oil and truffle salt, and of course regular olive oil and salt is just fine). A great light appetizer, or light meal with a salad.

When my son Luke was little, we would often go down to our dock on the Intracoastal Waterway off the island we lived on in S.C., and use a cast net to get enough shrimp for breakfast (Luke became very, very good at shrimping and crabbing and boating). If we went for shrimp later in the day, though, when the sun and dock were hot, any shrimp not put in the iced cooler right away very quickly became red (cooked) laying on the dock. A lesson for cooking; light touch.

Ingredients

1 to 2 lbs raw shrimp, shelled (any size works, but 16 to 20 count/lb is good)

1 sweet onion cut in quarters

2-4 lemons or limes, quartered

1-2 cloves garlic, crushed

Old Bay seasoning (to taste; at least several teaspoons)

2-4 fresh thyme sprigs

2 bay leaves

Dash or two of cayenne or other hot ground pepper

Salt and pepper

Olive oil (optional: some truffle oil or truffle salt)

Preparation

1. Add onion, lemons, garlic and spices to a large pot of water and bring slowly boil (slow to boil in order to let all the flavors out)
2. Add shrimp and bring just back to a light boil, then turn off the heat;
3. Pluck the lemons and onions out of the pot with tongs, then drain or quickly dip the shrimp out of the pot with a slotted spoon, and immediately plunge the shrimpinto a large bowl of ice water
4. After several minutes, remove shrimp with slotted spoon, to a serving bowl
5. Squeeze lemon juice on shrimp, then drizzle with a little olive (or truffle oil); sprinkle some salt (or truffle salt if you have it) and pepper over the shrimp, and serve.

-- surprising how tender shrimp can be –

<u>*Two: Pickled Shrimp*</u>

about 20 min prep, but needs to sit in fridge for several hours to overnight
serves 2 to 6

This recipe is adapted from chef David Link, who serves it in his HerbSaint restaurant in New Orleans (and now his Nashville restaurant Cochon Butcher). Beats all other pickled shrimp recipes I've tried. You can spice it up more by doubling the jalapeno, or by using serrano pepper (or even both). Shell the shrimp after pickling but before serving, and serve the shrimp nestled on top of the pickled veggies. Wonderful.

Ingredients

For the pickling mix

½ C diced turnip

½ C diced mushrooms (shitake best)

½ C diced carrot

1 jalapeno pepper, sliced thin (or use 2, or replace with Serrano pepper)

1 C red wine vinegar

2 T sugar

1 T salt (preferably sea salt, coarse ground or kosher)

1 T dried oregano

1 t crushed red pepper

1 t black pepper

[optional: 1 t grated or ground fennel, and some fronds if you have them for garnish]

For the Shrimp

8 C water

1 lb shrimp with shells on (16-20 count per lb is a good size, but any will do)

5 bay leaves

1 lemon, halved or quartered

1 T salt (preferably sea salt, coarse ground or kosher)

2 t cayenne

Preparation

1. First, make the pickling mix: combine all of the ingredients in a pot and just bring to a boil, while stirring. Remove from heat immediately and transfer to a bowl to let cool.
2. Then, for the shrimp, add all ingredients except the shrimp and bring the water to low boil (you can use the same pot you made the pickle in); add the shrimp, and when the water returns to a boil let cook for 1.5 to 3 mins, then scoop out shrimp and put them in an ice bath (a bowl filled with ice and water).
3. Drain the shrimp once cooled, and add to the pickle bowl. Cover and refrigerate for at least 2 hours (but can keep in the fridge for several days)

Shell the shrimp before serving, and serve on a bed of the pickled vegetables

VIKING WRAP VARIATIONS

grilled Lefse with various methods
20 min; serving size variable

My own creation, using the traditional Norwegian soft flatbread called Lefse. Like all good Norwegians and Norwegian-Americans, our family grew up eating Lefse, which is the Scandinavian equivalent of tortillas or pita bread or naan. Lefse is potato based (not flour) and has browned spots from cooking on a dry cast iron pan or stone. It is a soft flatbread perfect for rollups of any kind. You can find Lefse in most larger grocery store chains, usually near the cheeses, for some reason.

Since I try to grill almost everything (including fruit), one day I decided to lightly brush some Lefse with olive oil and grill it. What a wonderful discovery – it nicely changes both the texture and the taste of the Lefse, even after refrigeration. After that it was just a matter of experimenting with different fillings. The trick is to only grill a square (or half) piece of lefse (about 6" by 6") briefly on both sides, and to keep the fillings light, so it wraps or folds up fairly tight. Absolutely great appetizers served cold., and good for lunches or hikes.

These are my favorite variations. My favorite is not a rollup, though; but a square (see below)

Lefse Preparation

Cut the lefse in half (to create 6" by 6" squares)

Brush each square lightly with olive oil, on both sides

Grill quickly on 350 degree or so grill (about 30 to 60 seconds per side) use tongs to turn and remove to a plate

Set aside, stacked on a plate

Variations

Cream Cheese, Cucumber, Celery, Red Onion, /Scallions Shallots or Chives

Spread a T or so of soft or whipped cream cheese on a piece of grilled lefse

Add some thinly sliced cucumber or celery, and a little minced red onion or scallion

Adjust ingredients and amounts to taste

A little chopped Cilantro is also a good addition

Roll it up

Sliders

Grill some small (1/8 lb or less) burgers, from buffalo, elk, venison or beef)

Top with cheese and let melt

Place each mini-burger in the center of a 6" x 6" piece of grilled lefse

Fold in the corners of the lefse, and pin together with a toothpick

Serve immediately (while warm)

Very popular!

Buffalo Barbecue

Cook some ground bison (or beef, lamb or chicken); crumble or chop into small pieces

Add your favorite BBQ sauce, salt and pepper

Spread a T of BBQ along one half of a piece of grilled lefse

Add a bit of minced onion or shallot and roll up

Sour Cream, Avocado and Seeded Tomato: Self-explanatory; similar to above.

Lox and Cream Cheese

Like lox and bagels. Get thin sliced lox or smoked salmon, and soft cream cheese (use a bit more cream cheese than you would in the other related recipes). Add some capers if you like.

Smoked Ham and Cream Cheese Half Sandwiches

My favorite: smear about a T of soft or whipped cream cheese on a piece of lefse

Add some thinly sliced smoked ham, smoked salmon or lox to one half of the lefse

Fold in half, then cut in half again

The result is a nice 3" by 3" little finger sandwich...simple but very good, and great for parties

or snacks

With Hummus (of course)

-- riktig godt --

SIDE DISHES

(*also works as a Main Dish)

*Bhutanese Red Rice & Vegetable Stir Fry
*Broiled Shrimp (or Crab) & Salmon Cakes
Cauliflower mash
Collard Greens
Hoppin' John (Black Eyed Peas plus)
Mire Poix Stir Fry (with chicken, shrimp, tofu etc.)
Mushroom in a Red Wine Reduction
Norwegian (Norsk) Potatoes
Oven Roasted Carrots and Parsnips
Roast Asparagus with Tarragon and Cheese
Roast Butternut Squash & Red Onions
Steamed Carrots in Lime Butter with Pecan
Sufferin' Succotash
*Tomato Pie

BHUTANESE RED RICE AND VEGETABLE STIR FRY

20 to 30 minutes; serves 4

Due to alphabetical ordering, this recipe comes first under 'Side Dishes' (and one of those that double as a Main Dish), but the recipe is really the same as 'Mire Poix Stir Fry' listed below, the only difference being the use of Bhutanese Red Rice. The purpose of this entry, thus, is to remind you of the many different types of rice out there for you to consider and use.

Rice provides a significant amount of daily calories (protein and carbohydrates) for a majority of the world's population. Rice is the seed of a grass. Wild rice (Oryza sativa) is the progenitor of all strains of rice we use today. Rice was first domesticated in China some 13,000 years ago. From there it spread around the world, and various strains were developed. The majority of rice is still grown in Asia, but it has been grown in the U.S. (South Carolina) since the late 1600s, and is grown in the South, California and elsewhere in the U.S. today

All strains of rice are high in protein and calories, and rich in minerals and nutrients. All rice begins as brown rice; it is milled and polished to produce the more commonly consumed white rice. Generally, rice strains that are colored have more nutrients and antioxidant properties than white rice. Unless added in processing, rice has no gluten.

Some other grass species are also called 'rice' and popular in certain regions. American wild (or Indian) rice, for example, consists of four different species in the Zizania genus (not Oryza). Although related to Asian rice, Bhutanese red rice is also genetically distinct (like American wild rice), and it is the food staple in Bhutan, where it originates. Wild rice and Bhutanese red rice both have more nutrients than white rice, and they both have a more nutty flavor that white rice.

So, refer to the recipe for 'Mire Poix Stir Fry' below for ingredients and preparation, but try using wild rice or Bhutanese red rice or other types of rice, in all of your dishes that call for rice. If using white rice, our favorite is Jasmine.

BROILED SHRIMP (OR CRAB) & SALMON CAKES

20 to 30 minutes; serves 4 as main dish, or 8 for appetizers

I have made this recipe many times, and it always comes out great (even with stupid mistakes). It's easy and quick to make (as in 10 to 15 minutes active prep time; 30 minutes total with cooking). Great as appetizers, or as a main entrée. I recall that the original recipe came from a Seattle chef, as an alternative to the more ubiquitous crab cakes; I've altered it a good bit upon trial and error.

As Jess tells us, chefs pride themselves on being able to make better crab cakes (or shrimp cakes or salmon cakes) than anyone else, with the goal being to use as little binder as possible, so it's as much pure seafood as possible. In Beaufort, S.C., where we lived for a good while, the locals compete every summer to see who has the best recipe for crab cakes that year. They experiment with different, minimal binders (only beaten egg white instead of a whole egg; cornmeal or grits instead of breadcrumbs; different cuts of crab). Binder is the key, and this recipe makes it simple (yes, it uses a bit of mayo, but what is mayo but a simple emulsion of a little oil, egg and lemon juice?) As long as the cakes hold together on the plate, they're good (it's OK if they fall apart upon the first touch of a fork or knife). These 'cakes' hold together well, even if they come out lumpy, with almost nothing in them but seafood.

In light of the variations and experimentation noted above, you will not be surprised to hear that after several years of sharing this recipe, I changed my method: I cut the breadcrumbs and mayo in half, and now chop the shrimp and salmon into very small pieces. Or use crab, shredded (makes a nice NW local dish to use salmon or steelhead and Dungeness Crab) If you want more lumpy cakes, don't chop or shred as much, and double the amount of crumbs and mayo listed below (like I used to do). Try different versions and see which one you like best.

Ingredients

Roughly 8 oz of salmon (or steelhead) fillet

Roughly 8 oz large/jumbo shrimp, peeled [or crab, shredded into pieces]

1 large leek, white and light green parts only, quartered and chopped

[optional, but good] 8 oz shitake (or other) mushrooms, stemmed and chopped

1 egg

2 heaping T Panko breadcrumbs (very finely ground Japanese breadcrumbs; you can find in any grocery store)

2 heaping T (real) mayo

1 – 2T Dijon or honey mustard (I prefer the latter)

Dash (or more, to taste) cayenne pepper

Salt and pepper to taste

Olive oil as needed in first steps of prep

Preparation

1. Preheat oven to 375 degrees
2. Sautee chopped leek [and mushrooms if using] in a couple T of olive oil
3. Put shelled shrimp in bowl and drizzle with olive oil; salt and pepper, then toss
   a. If using crab instead of shrimp, sauté it in a bit of butter and set aside
4. Place salmon on baking sheet; rub both sides with olive oil; salt and pepper
5. Heat salmon in oven for about 4 minutes
6. Add shrimp to baking sheet (not touching salmon), for about another 5 minutes

a. Again, if using crab instead of shrimp, just keep the salmon or steelhead in the oven for another 5 minutes
7. When shrimp is pink or red, remove baking sheet from oven
8. Turn oven up to broil (with rack about 6" below heat)
9. Put egg, breadcrumbs, mayo, mustard and cayenne into bowl and stir; should be as thick or thicker than pancake batter (you can do this while the seafood is in the broiler)
10. Chop both shrimp and salmon into small pieces, and place into 'binder' bowl
11. Add leek and mushroom sauté to the mix, and stir (OK to use your hands)
12. Add more breadcrumbs, or more mayo, to adjust consistency
13. Adjust seasoning to taste (salt, pepper or cayenne)
14. Make cakes (large or small; they'll all be in dumpling shape; so press down lightly to flatten) and broil about 6 inches from heat source, for about 6 minutes (should be a bit of brown crust formed on top before you remove from broiler)

Presentation

Serve simply as appetizers, or as entrees on a bed of greens with a little vinaigrette and lemon wedge (tartar or aioli sauce if you want)

-- you will be surprised at how well received these simple cakes will be —

CAULIFLOWER MASH

15 min; serves 4

A low carb alternative to mashed potatoes (sometimes called 'mock potatoes'), but so good you may not even notice a difference. Very easy to make, but keep the boiled or steamed cauliflower as dry as possible before mashing or blending.

Ingredients

1 head of cauliflower

¼ C chicken stock

2-6 oz cream cheese

¼ to ½ C grated parmesan cheese

Chopped chives or green onions

Salt and pepper

[butter optional]

Preparation

1. Boil cauliflower forets (broken apart) for about 5 to 10 mins
2. Drain cauliflower, return to pot and add stock, cream cheese and cheese
3. Mash with a potato masher
4. Add cheese and greens; add spices

COLLARD GREENS

serves 4; about an hour

Collard greens are the most nutrient rich of all cruciferous (green leafy) vegetables (in the large and widely eaten family <u>Brassicaceae</u>). They have more potassium, vitamins A, C, D, fiber and phytonutrients than kale, chard, mustard greens or spinach. They grow almost anywhere, and they grow abundantly. We plant just two bunches in our garden each year, and they are both the first and the last thing we pick each season. If you cut the leaves about two inches above the ground they will grow a new crop in just another 2 to 3 weeks. Amazing. The leaves once cut are heavy and thick, almost like tobacco leaves. Of course, you don't have to grow them; you can find them in many grocery stores, and they are always cheap.

Sometimes generically referred to in the South as 'a mess of greens,' almost all recipes for collard greens call for some kind of fatty meat (bacon, bacon grease, smoked ham, ham hocks, etc.) Admittedly, they taste best that way, although we just use a bit of trimmed bacon (no grease) for our version. You can also just steam collard greens without any meat. Either way, we think it's best to tear or cut the leaves off the thick central stem in preparation, but some people (and restaurants) like to chop up and include the stems to add bulk. The stems are more bitter than the leaf, though, so we leave it out. The leaves get more tender the longer they cook (up to a point); about an hour at a strong simmer is plenty cooking time. Almost all recipes use hot sauce or pepper, and it truly does compliment this food stuff.

The term "pot likker" refers to the wonderful liquid left over from cooking collard greens. Some restaurants serve small sipping bowls of it as a stand-alone side. You can serve collard greens as a side dish by itself, or along with some black eyed peas or rice, or both. The next recipe, for "Hoppin' John" is a special mix of black eyed peas, and extremely good when served with collards.

Ingredients

2 T olive oil

6-8 slices thick bacon (smoked, preferably), cut into half inch chop

1 onion, chopped

2 cloves garlic, minced

1 C chicken stock; more to adjust as necessary while cooking

¼ C apple cider or red wine vinegar; more to adjust as necessary while cooking

3 bunches collard greens, rinsed

Several good splashes of your favorite hot sauce

Several good shakes of cayenne pepper

A bit of red chili pepper flakes

Salt and fresh ground pepper to taste

Preparation

1. Remove thick central stem from greens, and chop into 2" to 3" strips; set aside
2. Heat olive oil in deep soup pot; add bacon and cook over medium high heat for a few minutes
3. Add onion and continue cooking until translucent, about 3 to 5 minutes
4. Add garlic and stir for a minute
5. Add stock and vinegar, then add collard greens to pot and stir
6. Reduce heat to a simmer and cover; after about 15 or 20 minutes, when the greens have cooked down a bit, add hot sauce and spices, then cover and continue to cook at a simmer for another 45 minutes (for about 60 minutes total after you add the greens)

7. Then taste and adjust broth, vinegar and spices ... lots of room to tailor to your taste, but it should have a nice tart flavor of vinegar and a good bite of hot sauce/hot pepper

   -- great with rice or black eyed peas, or both –

HOPPIN' JOHN (FOR ALL SEASONS)

60 min (but only 10 min active); serves 4

This is a dish that came to the Carolinas and the Caribbean during slavery; it uses field peas or black eyed peas, as they were also cooked in Africa/Sierra Leone. Mary Rutledge, daughter of one of S.C.'s signers of the Declaration of Independence, recorded what may have been the first written recipe for Hoppin' John. It has since become known as a New Year's Eve dish, intended to bring luck (and when served as leftovers on New Year's Day in S.C., it's called 'Skippin' Jenny,' for no reason in memory).

Hoppin' John is usually mixed with rice, and served with collard greens and cornbread. The recipe below was created by a group of native South Carolinians on a New Year's Eve in our Atlanta condo many years ago. It doesn't use rice, and doesn't require pre-soaking of the peas, but it's damn good ... anytime. We usually serve collard greens and rice on the side, keeping the Hoppin' John to itself. And we __do__ serve it anytime!

Ingredients

2 T olive oil

2 stalks celery chopped

1 large sweet onion chopped

1 medium red pepper chopped (optional)

2 cloves garlic minced

5 to 8 slices smoked bacon diced

3 to 4 (breakfast style) pork sausage links diced

16 oz (1 pkg) black eyed peas (rinsed in cold water to sort out stones or floaters)

32 oz chicken stock

3 C water

2 bay leaves

chili pepper (1/4 t to ½ T, depending on taste)

salt and fresh pepper to taste

chopped Italian parsley for garnish (optional)

Preparation

1. In a 4 qt saucepan, heat oil and add onion, celery and pepper; cook about 10'
2. add garlic, bacon and sausage; cook about 2'
3. add peas, chicken broth, red pepper and spices
4. add about 3 C water; bring all to a boil, then reduce to simmer, cover and cook about 45'
5. Serve with collard greens and hot sauce on the side, and jalapeno cornbread (simply add diced jalapeno to cornbread mix). Excellent.

MIRE POIX STIR FRY (WITH CHICKEN, SHRIMP, TOFU ETC.)

15 minutes; serves 2 to 4

This recipe is nothing more than a simple mire poix, with mushrooms, that you add some protein to … cooked chicken, shrimp, or lamb, sautéed or grilled tofu or whatever. And some good herbs and salt and pepper to your taste: this is a quick 15 minute lunch or side or dinner. I make this often.

Ingredients

Note: the traditional ratio for mire poix, in order of 'onion to carrot to celery' is 2:1:1, but you can be approximate. I usually make about a ½" chop of each veggie, but you can experiment with a smaller (or larger) cut.

2-3 T olive oil

1 medium to large sweet onion, chopped

about 2 medium sized carrots, chopped

about 2 to 3 stalks of celery (ends cut off), chopped

6-10 oz protein (chicken, shrimp, lamb, tofu….)

1-2 t thyme (fresh or dried)

~1 t herbs de Provence

salt and pepper to taste

1 T balsamic vinegar (optional)

Preparation

1. prep any protein you plan to use (i.e., cook chicken or meat, shell shrimp or prepare tofu as you prefer), then chop into bite size pieces

2. heat a heavy pan (cast iron Dutch Oven works great) and add about 2 T olive oil
3. add the mire poix veggies and stir occasionally for about 5' to 7'
4. add some thyme (fresh or dried), other herbs and salt and pepper to taste while cooking
5. add mushrooms if using, and protein if using
6. cook a few more minutes, then add about 1 T balsamic vinegar (optional but recommended); let cool in pot without heat to evaporate vinegar if using

  -- *that's it. Good with or without rice, and good as leftovers* —

MUSHROOMS IN A RED WINE REDUCTION

15 to 20 minutes; serves 2 to 4

This recipe is from the Food Network chef Tyler Brown. It's a fairly standard approach to a simple wine reduction sauce, but ... oh yeah: it just happens to be fantastic! This can be served as a side dish all by itself, but it's really great with rice or fish of any kind, or as an omelet filling. Very nice flavors from the mix of mushrooms and the wine & stock reduction.

A variation of this works great in foil on the grill. Experiment (add cream after grilling).

Ingredients

2 lbs mushrooms, stemmed and chopped (try shitake, crimini, oyster, chanterelle, bella. Any kind works, but use at least 2 different kinds. 4 is even better).

2 shallots, chopped small (but not minced)

½ to ¾ C hearty red wine (Cabernet or Merlot is good)

¼ C beef stock

¼ C heavy cream (or half 'n half, but a bit thinner then)

2 T olive oil

1-2 T butter

1 heaping T of fresh thyme leaves

1 T minced chives (optional)

Salt and pepper to taste (holds pepper well)

Preparation

1. heat butter and oil in deep skillet

2. add shallots and cook at medium high heat until softened
3. add mushrooms and continue cooking, about 5' to 7'
4. add thyme, salt and pepper and mix
5. add wine and stir; cook until liquid largely reduced
6. add broth and stir; cook until all liquid largely reduced
7. remove from heat and add cream; mix and adjust salt and pepper

-- reheats well. Good to make ahead of time and reheat when needed –

NORWEGIAN (NORSK) POTATOES

30 min; serves 4

Something our mother made for special occasions; something you can find in Norway today. Usually called "Parsley Potatoes," but should be called "Butter, Cream Cheese and Parsley" potatoes. We would have this on special occasions (like when the Norwegian Lutheran minister would come to Sunday dinner), and us kids could eat as much as we want, as compared to any main or meat dish, which we were told to let the guests eat before the children took any. So we loved these potatoes!

Simple to do: parboil some cubed potatoes, then sauté in butter, add cream cheese and salt, pepper and parsley flakes. Easy, but so very good.

Ingredients
~ 1 lb oz new (or small) potatoes, cut into bite size pieces

~4 T butter

~4 oz cream cheese

Salt and pepper

Parsley flakes

Preparation
1. parboil cubed potatoes until just slightly tender to a fork
2. drain potatoes thoroughly, then put in a large pan with butter
3. cook potatoes over medium high heat until starting to brown
4. add cream cheese, salt and pepper
5. remove from heat and add parsley flakes, and serve

-- remember to let your guests eat the good stuff first —

OVEN ROASTED CARROTS AND PARSNIPS

45' to 60' (only ~10' active); serving size variable

I think my brother-in-law Don Rubin can roast root vegetables better than anyone in the world. I have proof: he has been doing it for years, and every time he does it, the result is both different and perfect. Just one of those people who has the knack. I have asked him how he does it. I have watched him do it. But I really cannot quite re-create it. Nonetheless, I try!

What Don says when asked (quixotically, of course), is exactly right: "just cut up some root vegetables; coat them in some oil, herbs and spices, and roast them in the oven at around 375 to 400 degrees for about 30 to 60 minutes." Simple, right? (simple if you like about a thousand possible variations within those guidelines).

But that really is the point with roasting root vegetables; there are so many possibilities. To help narrow and focus the options, here are a few additional tips:

> *First, 'root vegetable' is a broad category in itself, biologically including tubers, rhizomes, corms and bulbs. So start by limiting it to 'true roots,' or tubers. That brings you to the familiar food stocks of: carrots, parsnips, turnips, rutabaga, onions, potatoes and beets. Use this list to play around with at first, but note other roots you can roast include not only garlic, but also ginger, turmeric and others.*

> *Second, size of the cut: you need to keep the thickness of the veggies fairly consistent while roasting, in order to achieve a similar level of tenderness for eating. That gets modified by type of veggie, as some cook more quickly. You'll have to learn that by trial and error (or else call Don). My basic rule for doing a quick roast: make sure none of the veggies are more than about ¾" thick. They can be long (as in whole carrots), provided they are split lengthwise, if necessary, so they're about*

¾" thick. You can make a chop of veggie pieces all about the same size, or, as noted above, you can use the whole veggie and split or quarter it lengthwise. You will find that carrots get tender more quickly than parsnips, so you might adjust thickness with that in mind.

Third, coat the veggies in some canola, olive or sesame oil, adding salt and pepper, various dried herbs (parsley, sage, rosemary, thyme, maybe a dash of cumin or cayenne). You can also preheat some of the dried herbs in the oven, which brings out their flavors a bit more when you press or roll the veggies in them.

Finally, oven temp and cooking time: anywhere between 375 and 400 degrees is good; tougher veggies higher temp, and longer cooking time. It will take a good 30 minutes for any roast vegetable (even at 400 degrees), but it may take up to an hour. You can shorten that to as little as 15 minutes if you pre-cook on the stove top (recipe below). But however you cut and prep, check the veggies for fork tenderness while roasting. As noted below, you can pre-cook the veggies in a large oven proof skillet for a few minutes before putting in the oven (recipe below) which both shortens cooking time and helps with flavoring of the spices. And you can finish the veggies on the grill for extra flavor.

Ingredients

1 to 2 lbs carrots and parsnips, moderate size (cut to uniform thickness)

2-4 T oil (I use olive oil)

Variety of dried herbs and spices: parsley, sage, rosemary, thyme, salt and pepper, cayenne, cumin, oregano, Herbs d'Provence, etc.

[optional: melted butter for drizzling over finished product, or a vinaigrette]

Preparation

1. preheat oven to 375 degrees
2. drizzle some oil in a roasting pan or large bowl and rub cut veggies around to coat
3. sprinkle on your choice of dried herbs and spices and mix a bit more
4. put 1-2 T oil in a heated oven proof pan (I use a cast iron Dutch oven, uncovered) and place veggies in so that each veg is in contact with pan
5. cook for a about 2 minutes or so at medium high heat, then transfer pan to oven
6. roast for about 15 minutes and check for tenderness with fork
7. [note: you can skip the stove top step, but oven time will double]
8. Serve either by plate, or on a platter [optional: either drizzle a little melted butter over the veggies, or a little vinaigrette]

Putting the oven roasted veggies on the a grill for a few moments gets grill lines and adds flavor.

--wonderfully healthy and earthly flavor; experiment! --

ROAST ASPARAGUS WITH TARRAGON AND CHEESE

serves 4

As noted elsewhere, we have wild asparagus on our little ranch, so we experiment with many, many asparagus recipes every spring. This one is a perennial favorite with visitors, and us.

Ingredients

~1/2+ pound thin asparagus (pencil thin best); needs to be thin or won't cook enough

~2 T olive oil

1 large shallot, minced

~1 T fresh tarragon (packed tightly); torn into shreds

~1/4 t paprika (smoked paprika works great if you have it)

~3-4 oz shredded white cheese (Gruyere ideal, but Mozzarella fine)

sea salt and fresh ground pepper

juice of 1 medium lemon

Preparation

1. preheat oven to 450 degrees
2. break stem off bottom of one asparagus to see where natural tenderness ends, then cut remainder to that length
3. soak asparagus in cold water for 5 minutes; then drain and roll in paper towels to dry
4. in large, shallow baking dish, roll asparagus with the oil, shallot, tarragon, paprika, salt and pepper; spread out in single layer
5. roast for about 4 minutes

6. remove from oven; turn oven up to broil
7. add shredded cheese over asparagus (first dab up any little pools of oil with paper towel)
8. run under broiler just long enough to partially melt cheese; remove and turn off oven
9. add/adjust salt and pepper if desired
10. squeeze lemon juice over asparagus, and serve
11. [a great option is to cut the finished asparagus to small plate size, then serve with a poached egg or two on each serving]

-- tarragon and asparagus go together extremely well —

ROAST BUTTERNUT SQUASH AND RED ONIONS

35 to 40 min (5 – 10 active); serves 4 plus

A Thanksgiving recipe but incredibly good any time butternut (or other) squash are in season. Truly remarkable flavors for so few ingredients (and a great way to feature the healthy attributes of olive oil generally).

Ingredients

Large butternut squash (usually range from 2 lbs to 4 lbs)

One red onion for every lb of squash (so 2 lb squash = 2 red onions)

Olive oil (several T needed)

Pine nuts, dry heated in pan

Flat leaf parsley, coarsely chopped

Fresh black pepper and salt

Preparation

1. preheat oven to 475 degrees
2. cut ends off squash; cut in half and scoop out seeds; then cut off peel
3. cut peeled squash into ½ to 1" inch cubes
4. cut onions into 4 wedges from end to end, then peel (leaving root ends intact)
5. drizzle olive oil on two baking pans or dishes
6. arrange squash and onions separately on pans, with peel sides down; drizzle olive oil over all veggies (both sides), then sprinkle with salt and pepper

7. place in oven for 25 to 30 minutes; onions will likely be ready before the squash (remove from oven a bit early)
8. arrange squash and onions in a serving bowl or platter, then add parsley and pine nuts (and perhaps a dash of salt and pepper)

-- best eaten right away, but keeps well in fridge –

STEAMED CARROTS IN LIME BUTTER WITH PECAN

20 – 25 min; serves 4

Side dishes. Always good. This one is simple, and great.

Ingredients

2 T butter

1 ½ lbs carrots, sliced ½ in. thick on the diagonal (baby carrots work well)

2 green onions, thinly sliced

1-2 t finely grated lime zest (the skin of about 1 lime)

2 T fresh lime juice (about 1 lime – same one you skinned)

fresh ground pepper and ground sea salt

2 T chopped pecans

1 T chopped parsley

Preparation

1. Melt the butter in a large skillet; add the carrots and green onion
2. cook over moderate heat until green onions soften (about 3 min)
3. add lime zest, lime juice, salt and pepper
4. cover and cook until carrots are crisp tender (about 15 minutes)
5. stir in pecans and parsley

SUFFERIN' SUCCOTASH

20 min (only 10 active); serves 4

This is a more historically classic dish than most of us think. It is often thought of as a Southern food side dish, or associated with Thanksgiving. Both are correct, but the dish was long a staple of First Peoples on the east coast, a dish that just happened to be served at the very first Thanksgiving as a harvest meal. The derivation of the word "succotash" is from the Narragansett word "sohquttahhash," meaning 'broken corn kernels.'

The American Indian version of Succotash used corn and native beans (both domesticated early), and any other ingredients that were handy. Over the centuries the most popular added ingredients became onion, tomato and bacon, and lima beans (coming from Peru) were eventually replaced for native beans. All good.

This recipe comes from trial and error of the traditional ingredients, over many years. Good any time (not just Thanksgiving).

Ingredients

3-4 strips bacon, cut into ½" pieces (or to your preference)

1 medium sweet onion, finely chopped

1 to 2 cloves garlic, minced

2 C corn kernels (about 4 ears, or use frozen; I do)

1 C lima beans (I use frozen)

1 medium tomato, seeded (moist inside scraped out), cut into small pieces

~1 to 1 ½ C chicken broth

Salt and pepper to taste

2 T chopped flat leaf parsley (optional)

Preparation

1. Sautee bacon in large pan over medium heat until soft or browned (about 5')
2. Add onion and sautee for about 3-5'
3. Add garlic and sautee briefly
4. Add corn and lima beans; mix together
5. Add chicken broth (just enough to cover mix with broth) and bring to boil, uncovered
6. Reduce heat and simmer for about 5', or until corn and beans are tender
7. Add tomato
8. Adjust salt and pepper; add parsley and remove from heat

-- _"Sufferin' Succotash" was an epithet used by Daffy
Duck and Sylvester the Cat in cartoons_ —

TOMATO PIE

60 min (only 15 min active); serves 4 to 6

Tomato pie is a southern treat, especially during the summer when fresh tomatoes are plentiful. Unfortunately, like most Southern recipes, it's not exactly low cal. The original Beaufort, SC recipe that I followed called for 1 C mayo with 2 C grated cheese as pie topping, but I thought that was a bit extreme. So, this is a much lower calorie version (no mayo; skim milk cheese and less of it, addition of two beaten eggs and bread crumbs to thicken). I actually think this version tastes much better. [NB: total calories is less than 1200 for a pie (about 150 cal/slice), compared to over 3500 for the 'original' recipe]

Ingredients (for one pie)

4 to 6 medium tomatoes, sliced and seeded (take the moisture out to avoid a sloppy pie)

1 large sweet onion, sliced with slices chopped in thirds

1 pie crust

2 eggs, beaten w/about 2 T nonfat milk

1 ½ C lowfat grated cheese (cheddar/mozz mix is good)

½ to 1 C Panko bread crumbs

Dash of dried basil and oregano

Salt and pepper

Preparation

1. preheat oven to 350 degrees
2. press pie crust into pan
3. starting w/tomatoes, layer tomatoes and onions until pie is full (begin and end w/tomato layer)

4. sprinkle some salt and pepper as you build the layers, and a dash of the spices
5. beat eggs and milk w/fork; pour over pie
6. sprinkle grated cheese over the top
7. sprinkle Panko bread crumbs over cheese; dash more spices
8. bake uncovered for about 45' (bit longer for two pies at once)

-- you will be surprised at how much of a treat this is --

MAIN DISHES

(*also works as a Side Dish)

*Charleston Shrimp & Grits
*Ceviche (also makes Fish Tacos)
Chicken: Roast
Chicken: Spatchcock or Butterflied
Chicken Adobo
Chicken Pot Pie with Wild Mushrooms, Leeks & Tarragon
Green Peppers, Stuffed (with Elk, Buffalo or Venison)
Low Country Boil
*Quiche
Risotto with Chilean Sea Bass, Leeks & Mushrooms
Salmon with Mashed Peas and Tarragon Butter
Salmon, Braised with Crushed Grapes, Mushrooms & Mashed Potatoes
Shepherd's Pie
*Spinach Souffle
Steelhead (Poached or Steamed with lemon juice and herbs)
Thai curry (with shrimp or other themes)
True Torsk (baked cod fish)

CHARLESTON SHRIMP & GRITS

30 – 45 min; serves 4 to 6

I decided some time ago that it was unacceptable to have lived in the South for more than a decade and not have a good shrimp and grits recipe at hand. So with the help of chef son Jess and some research, we dug up the most traditional version around. I have since 'kitchen tested' this many, many times, and made slight adjustments. This is the authentic version, though; relatively quick (about 30 to 45 min) and absolutely, positively delicious. [Note: my sister Carol, then an official at CDC in Atlanta, asked if I would cook enough of this recipe to feed about 30 visiting health officials from around the world, for a dinner at her house -- all of whom wanted to sample 'authentic Southern cuisine'. We prepared several batches of this recipe, and it was a great success. The Health Minister from Thailand reportedly asked if she could recruit the chef to go back to her country with her!]

Charleston is the acknowledged home of classic shrimp and grits; the dish has been served there since at least the Revolutionary War, with very little change. New Orleans later added tasso ham in place of Andouille sausage, and although I must admit that tasso is superior, it's both hard to find (you can get good andouille at Publix, Safeway or Whole Foods) and not the traditional Charleston dish. There is actually a graduate school thesis topic lurking out there to track the different sources of andouille and tasso in the New World. South Carolinians claim andouille came to the Low Country with the French in the 1500s, and only later became known as a 'cajun' meat. Tasso pretty clearly did start in New Orleans, but then spread throughout the South. Another good thesis topic may lie in the fact that most 'Southern' cooking was simply 'homecooking' until the 1980s and 1990s, when it became trendy. Recipes from old diaries and parochial churches are the best guide to the real local food ... anywhere you are. This recipe came from old Charleston versions and diaries. Try it.

Ingredients

Grits

[Anson Mills in Charleston, S.C. has grits from heirloom grains; excellent source to order from]

3 cups milk

3 cups heavy cream

1 cup stone-ground white cornmeal (yellow will do; even Quaker grits will do fine, but 'instant' will not); the better the grits the better the dish [ignore cooking instructions on pkg; use these instructions instead]

2 tablespoons unsalted butter

sea salt and ground pepper

[NB: if you reduce the recipe, keep the ratio of milk/cream to grits constant ... I tried it with more milk than cream once, and it doesn't work]

Shrimp and Roux

2 tablespoons olive oil

1 medium white onion, minced (or white part of leek, or shallots, or combinations)

1 garlic clove, minced [optional]

~12 oz andouille sausage or tasso ham (or 1/2 and 1/2), cut in bite size chunks

1/4 cup all-purpose flour

2 cups chicken stock (or shrimp stock (using shells) or white wine or light beer, or combinations); a good choice is either all chicken stock or 1 1/2 C stock and

1/2 C beer)

2 to 3 bay leaves

about 1 3/4 to 2 pounds large shrimp, uncooked, peeled

cayenne pepper to taste preference

juice of 1/2 lemon

sea salt and ground pepper

2 tablespoons chopped flat-leaf (Italian) parsley

4 green onions, sliced

Preparation

Grits

Place a pot (3-quart minimum) over medium-high heat. Add the milk and cream. Slowly whisk in the grits. When the grits begin to bubble, turn the heat down to medium low and simmer, stirring frequently with a wooden spoon. Allow to cook for 10 to 15 minutes, until the mixture is smooth and thick. Remove from heat and stir in the butter (thin with extra cream if necessary). Season with salt and pepper.

Shrimp and Roux

1. While the grits are cooking, place a deep skillet or Dutch Oven over medium heat and coat with the olive oil (cast iron works best).
2. Add the onion and garlic; saute for ~2-5 minutes, or to soften.
3. Add the sausage and cook, stirring, until there is a fair amount of fat in the pan and the sausage begins to brown.
4. Clear a spot in center of pan and sprinkle in the flour [note: if there is not visible grease from the sausage, add a little butter in the center of the pan].

5. Stir with a wooden spoon to create a roux. Slowly pour in the stock and continue to stir the roux to avoid lumps.
6. Add the bay leaves, and when the liquid comes to a simmer, add the shrimp.
7. Poach the shrimp in the stock for 2 to 3 minutes, or until they are firm and pink and the gravy is smooth and thick.
8. Add the cayenne pepper and lemon juice. Season with salt and pepper; stir in the parsley and green onion (the parsley and green onion give it a nice pop).

Presentation

Spoon the grits into a serving bowl. Add the shrimp mixture on top (or do in layers, as I do) and serve. Stores and freezes well.

-- tradition and taste come together --

CEVICHE

15 min (plus 2+ hours in fridge); serves 4

What a wonderful dish. Ceviche (or cebiche, sebiche) most likely originated in Peru or Granada (Spain), or both. Wherever the point of origin (and it may have originated in multiple locations), humans discovered long ago that citric acids 'cook' fish effectively. Cultures along the coasts of southern Europe, Africa, Central and South America all developed local variations of this dish. With the advent of refrigeration, you don't have to eat it all right away nowadays (but it does get tough after a day). So many variations. This is just one, but a good one. It also provides the base for a great fish taco, so experiment.

Ingredients

about 2 lbs seafood (any whitefish, but salmon or tuna work, too;

my favorite is halibut or sea bass, scallops and shrimp), cut into half inch cubes

1 C lime/lemon juice (either or both: 50-50 is good)

1 C seeded and chopped tomato

1/2 red onion, finely diced

1 chile (jalapeno, poblano or serrano), seeded and finely diced

salt to tast

dash of cayenne or tabasco

Add as garnish to serve

chopped cilantro

sliced avocado

sour cream

salsa

chopped lettuce

Preparation

1. Mix all ingredients in ceramic dish and refrigerate; stir at least once to get acid mixing
2. Keep refrigerated for at least 2 or 3 hours before serving, or overnight (although note fish will get tougher after about 6 hours; still good, but just a bit more tough; you can drain off most of the liquid to slow the cooking if you want)
3. Drain juices before serving (or dip out with a slotted spoon)
4. Serve with cilantro, avocado, salsa, sour cream, chopped lettuce (some or all)

Fish Tacos

You can also use the ceviche mix and garnish for fish tacos, with 6" tortillas.

CHICKEN: ROAST

about 90 minutes; serves 4

Everyone who cooks needs a good recipe for roast chicken. The aromas from a roasting chicken fill a house like fresh baked bread, and the aroma from this recipe is exceptionally good. Adding a bit of white wine to the roasting pan near the end of cooking, at the same time that you raise the temperature of the oven, brings out incredible smells while helping to keep the bird moist and the skin crisp. Ending the roast with a hot temp helps make the skin toasty, and brings out the aromas of the chicken, ingredients and white wine even more. My notes show that when I first tried this approach I emailed my sister Carol (Sue) and said: "I'm roasting my weekly chicken tonight, with the porch doors open (beautiful full moon night), and the aroma is so damn good I thought I'd send you this particular variation (Jess and I have tried scores of roast chicken variations, but this one is very, very good, and the aroma is fantastic). Try it!"

So, … try it!

Ingredients

1 whole chicken (typically 4 to 6 lbs)

several T olive oil

seasoning (fresh chopped or dried):

    parsley

    sage

    rosemary

    thyme

    smoked paprika

    salt and pepper

1 lemon

1 onion, quartered

Cherry tomatoes (about a dozen)

white wine to cover bottom of pan (anywhere from 1 C to bottle)

Preparation

1. Preheat oven (or grill) to 350 degrees
2. Rinse chicken and pat dry (remove giblets and reserve for making chicken stock)
3. Coat both sides of the bird with olive oil, then sprinkle (both sides) with smoked paprika; chopped parsley, sage and rosemary; thyme; sea salt and pepper;
4. Put the bird on a rack in a roasting pan, then put a half lemon in the cavity, followed by some sprigs of rosemary and thyme, plus a clove or two of crushed garlic, and a few bay leaves (the little Turkish ones are best), followed by the other half of the lemon;
5. Place sweet onion wedges tossed in olive oil, salt and pepper around the bottom of the roasting pan, along with anything else you want (I've used sliced red pepper (great aroma), sweet potatoes, plum tomatoes sliced in half, etc.); add a few rosemary sprigs on the rack;
6. Put the roasting pan in the top third of the oven, and cook for 1 hour 15 minutes;
7. Remove soft vegetables like tomatoes, and add white wine to bottom of roasting pan to cover the bottom;
8. Increase heat to 450 degrees for another 20 minutes;
9. Remove from oven; let bird rest/cool for 15'. Remove veggies and serve separate. Delicious.

-- you can make a gravy by reducing the juices while adding a little flour and white wine and/or chicken stock --

CHICKEN: SPATCHCOCK OR BUTTERFLIED

45 minutes; serves 4

I was an Anthropology major in college (University of Chicago for two years, then Reed College in Portland, Oregon), and one of my Reed classmates wrangled a Watson fellowship to study at the Cordon Bleu in Paris after graduation. His proposal was to pursue aboriginal cooking techniques, which -- of course -- include grilling. His name was (is) Stephen Raichlen, and he now has a series of books on BBQ, and a PBS occasional series. One of the things I learned from Stephen's instructions is that the aboriginal method of cooking birds is technically called 'spatchcock.' It's simple: you remove the backbone of the bird, then turn it over and flatten it, so you can grill it more quickly, while retaining juices. The Big Green Egg borrowed this method for their cookbook, calling it 'Simon & Garfunkel' chicken ("Parsley, Sage, Rosemary & Thyme" as the primary herbs), and they get it just right. It is by far my favorite way to cook birds of any kind, and we spatchcock (or butterfly) a chicken weekly. Works great as a flavorful base for making chicken broth and chicken soup as well (see Soups).

I think this is best grilled, but it works in the oven as well (no need to turn the bird).

Ingredients

1 whole chicken (typically 4 to 6 lbs)

several T olive oil

seasoning (fresh chopped or dried):

   parsley
   sage
   rosemary
   thyme

smoked paprika

salt and pepper

Preparation

1. Preheat oven or grill (latter preferred) to about 375 degrees (can float a bit up or down if on grill)
2. Rinse chicken and pat dry (remove giblets and reserve for making chicken stock)
3. Use a sharp knife and kitchen scissors to cut out the backbone from the chicken (reserve for stock)
4. Turn chicken over and press down hard to break remaining ribs and flatten the bird to a butterfly shape
5. Rub olive oil over entire bird
6. Apply seasoning to both sides of bird
7. Cook breast side down for 20', then turn over and cook for another 25'
8. Let bird cool a bit and serve, either on a platter to cut at table, or cut up for individual servings
9. Reserve carcass and large bones for making stock.

-- this butterfly or spatchcock method is faster than roasting or grilling the whole bird. It produces a very moist bird, which works great in salads if you pull the meat --

CHICKEN ADOBO

2.5 hrs total (only about 15 min active); serves 4

A classic dish from Filipino cuisine, but really a favorite everywhere now. This is our version, distinguished by the liberal use of vinegar and by braising the meat to give it a rich and unusual flavor. There is a significant dispute in the Philippines about whether chicken, pork or beef makes the best adobo, so experiment (but adjust cooking times as necessary). Lots of variations on this recipe, but this one is good, and easy for the home cook.

"Adobo" is a term that originated in the Iberian Peninsula (now Spain), referring to a method of preserving meat. It used paprika, salt, vinegar, peppers, garlic and other spices for preservation of the food. Paprika has antibacterial properties, and it can break down fats allowing itself and the capsaicins in other peppers to penetrate more deeply into meat.

Magellan landed in the Philippines in 1521, beginning a long period of Spanish influence on the hundreds of islands that make up the country (the name "Philippines" was coined in 1543 in honor of then King of Spain Philip II). When Magellan arrived, his party found a native form of meat preparation that also involved vinegar and local peppers. So the Filipino version became called "Adobo," even though it was actually a different, Spanish dish. What we now call "Chicken (or beef or pork) Adobo" thus has both a Spanish and indigenous Filipino heritage, and it benefits from both.

A good way to serve this is to cut up or shred the chicken, put some pieces in a bowl over rice, then spoon the sauce over it all and serve with a spoon. Delicious.

Ingredients

1.5 C rice wine vinegar (or palm vinegar if you can find it)

1 C coconut milk

¾ C soy sauce

3 whole chiles (Birds Eye or anything hot)

3 bay leaves

Several cloves garlic, peeled

1.5 t freshly ground pepper

1+ t paprika

3-4 lbs chicken thighs (either skinless/boneless or not)

Preparation

1. Combine marinade ingredients (everything except the chicken) in a glass or plastic bowl (or a sealable plastic bag); add the chicken and coat the pieces
2. Refrigerate the chicken and marinade mix, sealed or covered, for at least 2 hours (overnight is even better)
3. Empty the chicken and marinade into a Dutch Oven or lidded pot and bring to a boil, then reduce to simmer and let cook, covered, for about 30 minutes, stirring occasionally
4. Turn on broiler; then remove chicken pieces from the marinade and put on a foil covered pan (for cleanup)
5. Bring the marinade sauce to high heat and reduce by half (about 10 minutes), until it has the consistency of cream (likely still be mostly liquid, but still great); then remove the bay leaves and chili peppers from the mix
6. Broil the chicken pieces for about 5 minutes, or until starting to caramelize, then remove pan, turn chicken and baste with marinade; return to broiler for about another 3 minutes
7. Remove chicken from oven and serve on a platter; drizzle the marinade sauce over the chicken, or serve in bowls over rice, with sauce.

-- a perennial favorite here; spice is nice --

CHICKEN POT PIE WITH WILD MUSHROOM, LEEK AND TARRAGON

about 2 hrs (but only about 15' active); serves 6 to 8

A very healthy chicken pot pie; loosely adapted from Food & Wine (March 2009). It's easy to make and unusually tasty. Leeks and tarragon make a great combination. Mushrooms pick up the pepper and make it a very basic, earthy taste. Add green peas (or edamame) and toasted almonds and this is a health food bonanza. Makes two pies or one deep casserole.

Ingredients

5 - 6 boneless, skinless chicken legs orthighs (~1.5 lbs)

1-3 t olive oil

2 T butter

1 sweet onion, 1/4 inch dice

1 leek (white and pale green), 1/2 inch pieces

8 oz. wild mushrooms (shitake work great, but any wild mushroom is better), sliced

1 T grainy mustard

1/4 C flour

1 C chicken broth

3/4 C whole milk

1/4 C heavy cream

2 T coarsely chopped tarragon

2 14 oz pkg pie crust (for top of pie only; no bottom)

1 C green peas (or edamame) (and carrots, celery ... whatever)

1/4 C almond slivers (or pine nuts), toasted (heated in a dry pan until browned)

1 egg/dash of milk (for egg wash)

Preparation

1. preheat oven to 400 degrees
2. sprinkle chicken with salt and pepper and olive oil; put in oven on baking sheet for 30' (save pan drippings)
3. cool and shred chicken
4. meanwhile, sauté onion, leek and mushrooms in butter, about 5'
5. whisk mustard and flour into veggie mix, cook about 1'
6. whisk in chicken broth, milk, half and half and pan drippings (may be up to 1/4 or 1/2 C; no worries), cook and stir about 5'
7. add chicken, tarragon, peas/edamame or other vegs, salt and pepper (heavy on pepper is good)
8. remove from heat and let cool about 30'
9. add toasted, slivered almonds (or pine nuts)
10. reduce oven to 375 degrees
11. spread mix in 8 x 11 deep dish (or similar size; a deep 8 x 8 in dish works great), _or_ in 2 pie pans (not full)
12. cover with pastry dough; adjust to fit (or not: I've made w/out a top crust)
13. cut three slits in dough; brush with egg wash (whisk an egg with a dash of milk for wash)
14. bake at 375 degrees for 45' to 60' (I do it in a covered dish, but not necessary)

A nice way to present this dish is in a braided dough: you can use pie dough or crescent roll dough. Lay out dough on foil placed on a sheet pan; leave 3" in the middle, then make cuts on either side about 1" apart. Place the pot pie mix in the middle, and fold the cut sides in, alternating. Cook as normal.

- -great dish. keeps well in fridge for several days --

GREEN PEPPERS, STUFFED (WITH ELK, BUFFALO OR VENISON)

about 1 hour; serves 4 to 6

These are wonderful tasting stuffed peppers, with lots of room for creativity (and available ingredients). You can make them vegetarian, or use meat. I like to use Elk or Buffalo, but that can be replaced with beef or lamb. This recipe serves the peppers as a whole, with the stuffing inserted from the cut off top. You can also do it by halving the peppers, though. We have several ranchers nearby who raise organic buffalo, elk and venison, but you can order great wild game from Nicky Farms out of Portland, at www. nickyusa.com

Ingredients

6 green peppers

1 lb ground Elk or Buffalo

1 medium sweet onion

1 clove garlic

1-2 T butter or olive oil

5 to 10 oz shredded mozzarella cheese

1 to 2 C spaghetti sauce

1 to 2 medium tomatoes, chopped

several T Worchester sauce

1 C cooked wild rice, brown rice or quinoa

dried basil, thyme and rosemary

salt and pepper to taste

Preparation

1. preheat oven to 350 degrees
2. cut tops off green peppers and scoop out seeds and membranes
3. boil peppers in large pot for 5 minutes; remove and drain
4. boil rice or quinoa
5. sautee onions/garlic/meat for about 5 to 8 minutes
6. add tomatoes and rice, and spices
7. put some salt in bottom of each pepper
8. on baking sheet, layer peppers with cheese, spaghetti sauce and onion/meat mix
9. top with sauce and cheese
10. bake for about 30 minutes

LOW COUNTRY BOIL (AKA FROGMORE* STEW)

about an hour; serves 4 to 6

This is an absolute standard in the South Carolina Low Country, prepared quickly with fresh caught shrimp and crabs, then poured out on plywood and sawhorse tables, covered in newspaper. We made this many, many times during the years we lived on a sea island off Beaufort, S.C. The recipe is meant to be approximate. Here's how I remember it:

- Sausage for 10 min. in a fast boil — [1/4 lb per person]
- Potatoes & spices for another 10' fast boil — [1-2 red pot. per person]
- Corn for 5' - 7', in a slow boil — [1 ear per person]
- Shrimp for 3' - 4' in a slow boil — [1/2 or more lb per person]

- Crabs, scallops or clams for 1' to 3' — [1/2 or more lb per person]

Ingredients *(for 4 to 6; adjust as necessary)*

1 lb Andouille sausage, sliced in ¾" pieces

4-8 red potatoes, quartered

4 ears corn, broken in half

2+ lbs raw shrimp (shells on)

2+ lbs whole crabs, scallops or clams

Old Bay seasoning to taste (several Ts)

Preparation

1. Bring a large stockpot, slightly more than half full of water (not full), to a rolling boil
2. Add Andouille sausage, cut into 2" links (any smoked sausage will do -- but spicey all the better) [about 4 lbs for 16 people]
3. continue fast boil for 10 minutes
4. Add 16+ small red potatoes, cut in halves (or equivalent medium potatoes, quartered);
5. Add "crab boil" spices (best is 1 or 2 "Old Bay" Crab Boil packets -- spicey all the better, but use mild for kids);
6. Add several lemon quarters, and a clove or two of garlic
7. continue fast boil for another 10 minutes
8. Add corn [about 1 ear/person], broken into halves;
9. reduce heat to a slow boil for 5 - 7 minutes
10. Add 4-8 pounds shrimp;
11. continue cooking for only 3 - 4 minutes (just until the shrimp turn red)
12. Drain and serve on a large platter, or on an outdoor table covered with newspaper

* Frogmore was an old plantation on St. Helena Island, SC (the sea island just south of Lady's Island, where we lived). The Low Country Boil tradition started there.

QUICHE

45 – 55 min (15 min active); serves 4 to 6

This recipe works for just a cheese, or cheese and mushroom quiche, or for other ingredients. We are blessed at the Gorge Ranch to have wild asparagus every spring. It is so abundant from mid-March through April that we have to keep thinking of different ways to prepare it. So we make wild asparagus quiche several times every spring, that looks as good as it tastes.

Ingredients (for 2- 8" pies)

[optional: if using asparagus, take about 1 lb (24 stalks), thin is best, and snap stems to find natural cut; save a dozen tops cut to 4" for topping; chop the remainder to 1/2" pieces

2 - 8" pie shells (prepared pie crusts fine)

10 slices bacon, cut into ½" pieces

1 shallot or ½ onion, chopped

6 eggs

2 C half and half

2+ C grated cheese (use diff varieties: mozz, goat, cheddar, etc.)

8+ oz wild mushrooms

1 to 1.5 T flour

Dash nutmeg; salt and pepper (and rosemary, thyme or tarragon: optional)

Preparation

1. Preheat oven to 400 degrees
2. Put pie shells in pie plates; stab with fork all over bottom

3. [if using asparagus: steam tops for about 4'; drain and cool]
4. Cook bacon, cool and crumble (or chop before cooking)
5. Sauté shallot, mushrooms and chopped asparagus (in bacon grease or a little olive oil)
6. Beat eggs in bowl; add half and half and spices, flour and stir
7. Layer bacon, [chopped asparagus if using], bacon, onion and then cheese in pie
8. Pour egg and cream mix over pies
9. [if using asparagus, arrange the 4" steamed tops in a wheel on top of each pie, tips facing toward edge]
10. Bake for about 30' to 40'

-- let cool and serve. looks good, tastes good. all good --

RISOTTO WITH CHILEAN SEA BASS, LEEKS & WILD MUSHROOMS

30 - 45 min; serves 4

I love risotto and searched (and tried) a dozen recipes before simmering it down to this. My chef son Jess tried it and said he was shocked (because it was so good). He says good risotto is actually hard to make correctly, consistently ... but this one does it. You can substitute scallops or salmon for the sea bass, or just make it plain. Sea bass really seems to work the best, though. The key is to keep stirring throughout the 25 minutes that the rice mix simmers, which is why it's hard to do well consistently; takes some attention.

Ingredients

5 cups fish stock (or bottled clam juice)

2+ T olive oil

1 lb leeks, white part only (about 4 large leeks); quartered lengthwise and chopped

4 green onions (including some green part); sliced

2 cloves garlic; minced

1 1/2 C risotto rice (arborio or medium grain variety)

1 C white wine (dry)

1 1/2 lb chilean sea bass; skinned & filleted; cut into 1 1/2 inch pieces

1/2 to 1 lb wild mushroom mix (or just shitake); sliced

3 T minced rosemary

Sea salt and ground pepper

2 T grated lemon zest

Preparation

1. Bring fish stock to boil in sauce pan; reduce to simmer
2. In large saucepan or pot, heat olive oil over medium heat, then add leeks, green onions and garlic, and sauté until wilted (about 3 min)
3. Add rice and stir until opaque (about 2 min)
4. Add wine and stir, until nearly evaporated
5. Add ladleful of simmering stock and stir, until nearly absorbed (about 3 min)
6. Continue adding stock like this, while stirring (about 25 min total)
7. Meanwhile, sauté the mushroom mix in some olive oil, and set aside
8. When rice is al dente, add fish cubes and mushrooms
9. Add rosemary, salt and pepper, and stir gently for 3 to 6 minutes (enough for fish to cook)
10. Stir in grated lemon zest and serve

SALMON WITH MASHED PEAS IN TARRAGON BUTTER

20 to 30 min fridge to table; serves 4

This has become one of my favorite ways to make salmon. A truly remarkable recipe (base recipe from Food & Wine magazine, April 2014). Tastes far more complex that you would think from just looking at the ingredients. Yes, the recipe does call for a tad of cream and some butter (which is undoubtedly why it tastes so damn good), but try it. It is surprisingly quick to make, and it is a meal in itself. Well, maybe serve with some bread (or rice and mushrooms — see below), but protein and greens right there on one plate.

Note: if you only make a half recipe, use the full amount (16 oz) green peas. The original recipe was light on the green peas, so use 2 lbs peas if making 4 servings. Also, I've used regular milk instead of cream, and it really didn't affect the flavor or texture that much, so there's that.

Ingredients (serving for 4; adjust if different)

2 lb (32 oz) frozen peas (hey, it's easy)

4 6-oz salmon fillets with skin on

1 C dry white wine

½ C heavy cream (but I've used regular milk, too)

7 T unsalted butter

2 T chopped fresh tarragon

2 t lemon juice

Salt and pepper to taste

Preparation

Three separate preps required here: (1) peas; (2) sauce, and; (3) salmon. You can do all three overlapping. Easy.

Mashed Peas

1. Boil water in large pot and add peas; cook at boil for about 3-4'
2. Drain peas and reduce heat to pot; add 1 T butter and the ½ C cream; then add peas back
3. Mash peas with potato masher; season w/salt and pepper and set aside (keep warm or reheat)

Tarragon Butter Sauce

1. Meanwhile, in small sauce pan simmer the 1 C wine and 2 t lemon juice until reduced to about 1 tablespoon
2. Reduce heat and add 6 T butter, ½ or 1 T at a time, until melted; whisk in tarragon, salt and pepper
3. Set aside (keep warm or reheat)

Salmon (or Steelhead or Trout)

1. While doing the above, heat a pan (cast iron grill pan works great, but any will do)
2. Rub salmon with the olive oil and season with salt and pepper
3. Cook salmon skin side down first, for about 6-7'; then other side for about 4-5' (only turning once)

Presentation

Spoon the mashed peas onto plates and top with salmon, skin side up (or, if grilling or using a grill pan, the salmon looks pretty with grill marks up and skin side down). Spoon tarragon butter sauce over the salmon and peas, and serve. Delicious.

This is a meal by itself, but also works well to serve with wild rice (or any rice) and a Red Wine and Wild Mushroom Sauce (see recipe under Side Dishes).

-- this really is a meal in itself, and so good --

SALMON, BRAISED WITH CRUSHED GRAPES, MUSHROOMS & HORSERADISH MASHED POTATOES

45 min; serves 3 to 4

This recipe is from the chef at Wildwood Café in Portland Oregon, which sadly is no longer in operation. He used grapes from Willamette Valley vineyards during first crush in the fall, which made this a very popular dish there seasonally (but great any time). Visually impressive, and tastes even better. (This is really closer to poaching than braising, but I'll defer to the chef's description). I served this to several visitors from both NYC and the Pacific NW one time, and they all liked it.

Ingredients

3 to 4 salmon steaks (or fillets)

2 T olive oil

2+ C white grape juice

1/4 C chardonnay

1 small red onion, sliced into crescents

1 C seedless green grapes

1/4 C minced flat parsley

2 T lemon juice

2 T butter

1 - 2 lbs Yukon Gold potatoes; quartered

2 - 4 T cream cheese

2 T butter

2 - 4 T horseradish

1 C milk

Preparation

1. Preheat oven to 350
2. Boil water for potatoes and simmer for 15 to 20 min
3. In ovenproof skillet, heat oil and add salmon; season w/salt & pepper and brown on both sides (3 to 6 min)
4. Remove salmon; add wine, grape juice, grapes and onion; bring to simmer
5. Return salmon to skillet, then transfer to oven
6. Braise for about 10 to 20 min (depending on thickness of salmon)
7. Remove salmon from skillet; bring sauce to simmer and reduce; stir in parsley, butter and lemon juice;
8. Mash potatoes with butter, cream cheese, milk and horseradish

Presentation

Serve with mashed potatoes; setting salmon on top; covered with sauce; pair with a good Chardonnay.

SHEPHERD'S PIE

45 – 60 min; serves 2 to 4

One of the times that my dear friend and law partner Larry Bracken (of Irish descent) came to visit the Gorge, I decided to try a traditional Irish recipe. I scanned several recipes on the web, then mixed and matched and tried this. Turned out pretty good (except I added way too much cayenne when Larry was here ... sorry!) It appears that most Americans use ground beef instead of lamb when making Shepherd's Pie, which is then more appropriately called 'Cottage Pie.' Don't do that: millions of Irishmen (and coyotes) can't be wrong; lamb is VERY good, and much more lean than beef. Larry told me a great story about an older Irish relative who didn't like Shepherd's Pie when presented, saying that 'once you've been a shepherd for years and years, you no longer want to eat this!' But for those of you non-shepherds out there, this is a meal to itself, and very, very good.

Ingredients

For the mashed potatoes (the topping)

2-3 medium to large Yukon Gold potatoes, cubed

small amt milk or cream (few ounces)

2-4 T butter

2-4 T cream cheese (fat free works well)

For the mix (the 'pie' itself)

Mire Poix:

> 1 sweet onion, diced
> carrots: ½ onion amt, sliced
> celery: ½ onion amt, sliced

8-12 oz mushrooms (Shitake good)

2 T olive oil

1 lb ground lamb

2-4 T butter

2-4 T flour

1/2 to 1 C hearty red wine (as in Merlot, Cabernet or Syrah), _or_ (not 'and') chicken or beef broth …

herbs (parsley, rosemary, thyme)

salt and pepper

[I put a good sprinkle of cayenne pepper in it, which is good, but ONLY if a sprinkle!]

For the finish (on potato topping before going into the oven)

several oz parmesan cheese

1-2 t or so Worchester sauce

Preparation

1. Preheat oven to 400 degrees
2. Boil potatoes until tender; drain; mash with milk, some butter and cream cheese; set aside
3. Saute mire poix and mushrooms in 2 T of olive oil
4. Add lamb to mire poix once the veggies are tender, and stir until lamb no longer pink
5. Clear spot in middle of pan, add butter then stir in flour, and slowly add wine or broth while stirring to make a roux
6. Add spices
7. Put veg/lamb mix in small casserole dish, cover w/mashed potatoes

8. Sprinkle parmesan cheese (and a few drizzles of Worchestershire) on top
9. Bake at 400 for 20-30 minutes (place a cookie sheet or other pan underneath to catch drippings)

-- eat the pie, but keep an eye on the flock --

SPINACH SOUFFLE

(aka "Suedon Souflle")
about 75 min; serves 4 to 6

No, this is not some exotic Thai recipe (although 'Suedon' does sound exotic): it is a delicious and fool proof soufflé pioneered by my dear sister Carol Sue and dear brother (in-law) Donald Lutan (perhaps it should be called 'SueLutan'?). They made it while nursing me back to recovery after some surgery, and the recipe has been tested on my other dear sister Shari and dear brother (in-law) Howard (who watched over me through surgery and hospital), as well as on many family members and friends. We came up with this version by surfing the internet (me on morphine recovering) and reading different recipes aloud, then mixing and matching what sounded best. I have since tried and adjusted it several times. Delicious and fool proof (and I am just the fool to prove it). Try it!

Ingredients

1 medium to large sweet onion (Vidalia, Walla Walla, Mayan, etc.); chopped

6 eggs, separated (yolks beaten; whites whipped)

5 C (packed) spinach (or 1 large spinach container from store); blanched and chopped

1 C grated parmesan cheese (or mozz)

2 C milk (I use organic nonfat)

4 T flour

4 T butter

olive oil for sautéing onion

salt and pepper to taste

Preparation

1. preheat oven to 350 degrees
2. sauté chopped onion
3. boil water to blanch spinach (put in boiling water for 1-2', then drain and chop)
4. measure and set aside all other ingredients (mise en place really helps with this recipe)
5. whip egg whites (fork works, but egg beater is better; thick but no peaks)
6. make white sauce:
   -- melt the 4 T butter in large/deep pan
   -- slowly stir in 4 T flour to make a roux
   -- slowly stir in 2 C milk to make sauce; stir until no lumps
   -- add salt and pepper to taste
7. keep heat low and quickly add other ingredients to white sauce, stirring in: onions, spinach, egg yolks, cheese and egg whites
8. adjust salt and pepper to taste
9. grease deep dish with some butter or olive oil, then add mixture
10. place baking dish in pan of water, then put both in oven; cook uncovered for 45 to 50 minutes

... and voila! serves 4 to 8 (or 2 college students). very low cal, as in about 160 cal per serving if 8 servings. crispy onions are a perfect garnish if you have them.

THAI CURRY (WITH SHRIMP OR OTHER THEMES)

30 minutes fridge to table; serves 4

Almost everyone loves good curry, whether with shrimp, scallops, chicken or tofu. I sampled my favorite Thai and Indian curries, and tried many different recipe variations before coming up with this incredibly quick and authentic version. My son Jess (former chef who has spent a lot of time in the Near East), is amazed at how good – and quick – this is to make. The list of ingredients looks daunting, but it's not. Just set up the spices ahead of time, with a teaspoon set by them. Do the prep on the other 4 or 5 ingredients before you start cooking, and it comes together remarkably fast. You do need to find coconut milk, but even the local grocery in the cowboy town near us now carries that. My sons request this dish more than any other when we all get together for a few days.

Ingredients

2 – 4 T olive oil

1-2 lb (depending on how much you want) raw, shelled shrimp (frozen and thawed works fine;

16 – 20 count per pound is a good size); cut to bite size pieces [or substitute cooked chicken, scallops, tofu]

1 medium to large size sweet onion, sliced and cut into ¾" (or so) pieces

couple of cloves of garlic, peeled and sliced thin

a few slices of fresh ginger is good, but optional

8 to 10 oz mushrooms (shitake good, but any kind fine), stemmed and cut into large pieces about a dozen or more snow peas or snap peas, ends clipped and cut into 1" (or so) pieces

spices: 1 t (or more depending on your palate) each of the following

curry
cumin
turmeric
ground red pepper
paprika

plus several good shakes of cayenne pepper (to your taste)
plus salt and ground pepper (to your taste)
pinch of dried thyme, rosemary (Herbs de Provence if available)

1 16 oz can of coconut milk ('lite' if available; can be found in most large grocery stores)

1 16 oz can diced tomatoes (or dice them yourself)

several T chopped Thai basil (regular basil OK)

several T chopped cilantro

Preparation

1. Heat large skillet and add olive oil; sauté onion for about 5-7' (until softened), then add mushrooms and garlic, and cook to soft (about 10' total)
2. Pull skillet off heat and let cool while adding spices; stir the spices into onion/mushroom mix
3. Return to medium heat, add coconut milk and diced tomatoes and stir; add snow peas and ginger (if using), bring to simmer and cook, stirring occasionally, for about 7'
4. Add shrimp or other protein, basil and cilantro and cook for about 2-3' more
5. Adjust spices, then serve with rice, cous cous (Pearl cous cous my favorite with this dish) or other side.

-- this is a quick dish that tastes great, and gets even better as leftovers --

TRUE TORSK (BOILED AND BROILED COD FISH)

15-20 min; serves 4

Torsk means "cod fish" in Norwegian, and Norwegians have used torsk as a staple food for centuries. There are several species of cod fish in the Gadus genus (and fishmongers often market other types of white fish as "cod," but you will often see "True Cod" labeled in the store, or even the Norwegian word "Torsk"). True cod lives in the cold waters of the northern Atlantic or northern Pacific. It is a rather bland fish, but high in protein and easily prepared by various methods.

One of the more unusual preparations of cod is the Norwegian tradition of "lutefisk," where cod is dried for storage, then reconstituted in a mixture of water and lye (traditionally the lye came from the ashes of burned birch trees). The traditional utility of lutefisk was that it was a source of protein that kept for long periods of time, and through hard winters. When reconstituted for consumption, however, it requires thorough rinsing to get out the lye, and the meat usually falls apart into pieces. Those pieces are then boiled, drained and served with melted butter. Lutefisk has never really been a menu item in Scandinavia, but it's historic utility is still celebrated as a holiday tradition, and our family has enjoyed (endured?) lutefisk for many, many decades ... only once a year. It does make your kitchen smell bad because of the lye, however, and few people really enjoy it (sorry, min foreldres og besteforeldres).

This recipe may be somewhat reminiscent of lutefisk, because it involves boiling cod and the use of melted butter, and it sometimes falls apart a bit. But it will not make your kitchen smell bad, and it honestly tastes like lobster when finished. So make this your "Lutefisk Alternative" Norsk Amerikaners!

In this recipe you boil the cod briefly in water with salt and sugar, to break down some of the tough connective tissue and pre-cook the meat. Then you

184

drain the fish, add some melted butter and spices, and broil for just a few minutes. That's it; simple. It can be made quickly, and even though it is a bit of a strange recipe, it is extremely tasty. Try it!

<u>Ingredients</u>

4 – 6 oz pieces of fresh cod

about 4 C water

about 4-6 T granulated sugar

about 1-2 T salt

about 4-6 T butter, melted

paprika

dash cayenne or ground chipotle chili

salt and pepper

<u>NOTE</u>: *this is not baking, so none of the above measurements need be precise. The salt/sugar water is used solely to break down tough tissue, and you can't go wrong with the amount of butter, so don't worry about precise measurements on any any of this, just go by instinct and taste.*

<u>Preparation</u>

1. Mix the water, salt and sugar in a saucepan, then place the cod in the pot (with enough water to just cover the fish … add water, sugar and salt as needed to cover; nothing magic about the ratios)
2. Bring the water/fish mixture to a boil and continue boiling for about 3 minutes (this pre-cooks the fish and makes the fish more tender)
3. Meanwhile, melt the butter in a small pan and set aside with a spoon for drizzling

4. Turn on the broiler in your oven (I use 'hi' setting with the rack about 6" from the heat source)
5. Remove the fish from the water mixture (be careful not to break the fish pieces apart if you can), and pat dry with paper towels, then put on a baking sheet covered with aluminum foil (for easy cleanup)
6. Drizzle some of the melted butter over the fish, then sprinkle some salt and pepper, paprika and just a dash of hot pepper over it all
7. Broil for about 5 minutes, or until the fish looks browned and delicious
8. Remove from oven and drizzle remaining butter over fish.

-- goes well with Norsk Potatoes or rice (and salad); truly tastes like lobster --

DESSERTS

Chocolate Mousse
Frozen Yogurt Sundaes with Grilled Pineapple and Toasted Pine Nuts
Norwegian Krumkake
Panna Cotta with Wild Berry Preserves
Poached Pears in Red Wine
Norwegian Almond Cookies

CHOCOLATE MOUSSE

only 10 min prep, plus at least 2 hrs in fridge to set
serves 4

A simple but delicious dessert, and a perennial favorite with our clan. There are lots of exotic recipes for chocolate mousse out there, but this one keeps it simple on purpose. There are only 3 ingredients, so it's about the quality of those ingredients, and careful prep. Serve as is, or with a dab of whipped cream on top (but that's really not necessary). Delicious. (Note: you can experiment with lots of different versions of this, but a couple of easy things to try are (1) add some coarse salt to the mix; and/or (2) add a dash of cayenne or ground chipotle chili pepper). Salt and hot pepper both bring out the chocolate flavor more intensely, without being individually noticeable. A shot of rum is also good, but that is more noticeable (albeit in a good way).

I made this for a large dinner with friends recently, using a mix of chocolate bars with hazelnuts, caramel and coconut, and it was great.

Ingredients

5 oz semisweet (or bittersweet) chocolate, coarsely broken into pieces (Lindt's or Ghiradelli from the grocery store works fine; the better the chocolate, the better the mousse)

1 C very cold heavy cream (put in freezer for a few minutes before starting recipe)

3 egg whites (no yolk)

[optional: dash of coarse salt or cayenne/chili pepper, or both]

[optional: 1 oz. rum]

Preparation

1. Make a double boiler to melt the chocolate pieces with ¼ C of the cream (then return the cream to the freezer until you use it in the next step) [double boiler means putting a heat proof bowl with the ingredients inside of a pot with a few inches of water in it, ideally keeping space between the water and the bottom of your ingredient bowl]

2. Stir the chocolate and cream with a spatula until melted and well blended, then remove and let cool some while completing remaining steps

3. Whip the 3 egg whites in an electric mixer until you get stiff peaks (about 1-2 minutes)

4. Clean off the mixer beaters and whip the remaining ¾ C cream in a separate bowl, until you get stiff peaks of whipped cream (about 3 minutes)

5. Using a clean spatula, slowly stir the whipped cream into the melted chocolate

6. Gently fold the whipped egg whites into the mixture, until well mixed (but don't over stir)

7. Spoon the mousse mix into ramekins, small bowls or wine glasses, cover with plastic wrap and refrigerate at least two hours (but will keep several days)

-- about 350 calories per serving, and worth it! --

FROZEN YOGURT SUNDAES WITH GRILLED PINEAPPLE AND TOASTED PINE NUTS

about 10 to 15 min; serving size variable

Invented this out of necessity for Luke's high school prom dinner; 4 young couples all dressed up, sitting outside in our beautiful River Room (roof and floor and huge beams, but open air) on an island along the IntraCoastal Waterway in S.C). Dad was cooking, but I forgot about dessert. So this was done on the fly, and has since become a family favorite. It's extremely popular after large dinners, but plan to keep making them, as guests will want seconds.

Ingredients

Fresh pineapple, cut into 1" thick rounds, and brushed with olive oil

Frozen yogurt or vanilla ice cream

Pine nuts

Preparation

1. Grill the pineapple slices (brushed with olive oil) for several minutes on each side, enough to heat and get grill marks
2. Meanwhile, toast the pine nuts in a dry pan until nicely browned, while stirring or shaking, then remove from heat
3. Remove pineapple from grill and cut into 1" squares
4. put scoops of vanilla yogurt or vanilla ice cream in clear glasses or wineglasses
5. add grilled pineapple pieces to each glass, then sprinkle some toasted pine nuts on top and serve

*-- the pineapple and pine nuts melt a nice glaze
on the yogurt or ice cream: delicious --*

NORWEGIAN KRUMKAKE

~75-90 mins; makes about 42 (allowing 6 for trial and error)

OK, so this is an unusual recipe to include, because it requires a special small griddle, it is decidedly ethnic and it is usually considered to be only a holiday treat. But in an effort to ensure that my sons, extended family and friends will recall this treat from our Norsk heritage (and hopefully keep the tradition going), I am including it. You can find a Krumkake griddle on line quickly, and they are reasonably priced.

In Norsk, Krumkake means "bent or curved cake," and it is just that; a very thin waffle cake that is rolled into a cone. When they cool they become crisp. They can be eaten as is, or filled gently with some whipped cream or a little fruit. I prefer to dip the narrow end in melted chocolate. They are tasty (also fragile), but a true tradition for Norwegians and Norwegian-Americans. This recipe comes from Grandma Dee (and our great grandmothers Elise and Asa and Kari and beyond), adjusted slightly from experience.

This recipe takes some time to complete, but it is fun with kids, and another session of cooking as meditation. Some common problems: if the first krumkake come out white and/or rubbery, your heat is too low. If the first ones come out dark brown, the heat is too high. Your goal is to keep them lightly browned, so you can see the pattern from the waffle iron.

Another tip: stick to the roughly 30 seconds per side. Either track a watch with a second hand or simply count to 30 (that is what I do). Flip the iron once after 30 seconds, then flip it again after another 30 seconds and open to remove the waffle with a thin metal spatula. If you do that, the side facing you when you open the iron with still be pale (it's been facing the heat only 30 seconds), while the bottom side will be nicely browned. Roll the waffles up on the wooden cone immediately upon removing from the iron, because they start to harden within a few seconds. Then repeat....40+ times!

Ingredients

3 eggs

4 T butter, softened

1 C sugar

1 C whole milk (or Half 'n Half, cream not necessary)

½ t nutmeg

a few to several drops of vanilla and/or almond and/or lemon extract

~1 ½ C flour

Preparation

1. Preheat krumkake griddle on medium high (then lower when you begin a batch)
2. Cream the butter into the sugar in a medium bowl
3. Stir the eggs into the mix with a spoon, one at a time, and mix thoroughly
4. Stir in the milk and any extract you chose (vanilla/almond/lemon)
5. Slowly add the flour and stir; it should look and feel like a fairly thick pancake batter when ready
6. Turn heat under griddle down to medium, and test with water until droplets sizzle
7. Spoon 1 T of batter onto griddle and close (wipe off any excess on the sides with a paper towel); NB: you will actually only get about 2 t of batter on the iron, because the rest will stay on the tablespoon
8. After about 30 to 45 seconds, turn the griddle over [NB: the first few cakes almost always come out dark; takes a bit to 'season' the griddle]

9. Remove the waffle from the griddle with a small metal spatula, lay on counter and roll up over the wooden tapered dowel that comes with the griddle

10. Start the next krumkake while the preceding one cools; take cooled waffle off the cone and put on rack, and the continue the process

11. [optional] I like to dip the narrow end in melted chocolate, and set aside on waxed paer until they cool; so good....(but a little whipped cream in the large end is good, too)

-- pass it on....

PANNA COTTA WITH WILD BERRY PRESERVES

about 15 min active, but 3 hours in fridge; serves 4

Italian for 'cooked cream,' Panna Cotta is a simple dish from northern Italy, served with berries, caramel or chocolate, usually in small portions. You can serve it in ramekins or small bowls, or invert and remove from bowl. This is a quick and pleasing recipe that can be used either as an appetizer or as a light dessert.

Ingredients

1 quart heavy cream

1/2 C sugar

1 vanilla bean, split and scraped

2 1/4 t powdered gelatin

3 t water

berries (Polana black currant, or any whole preserves, work well)

Preparation

1. combine cream, sugar and vanilla bean and seeds in pan; bring to simmer over moderate heat; then remove from heat, cover and let sit 15'
2. meanwhile, sprinkle gelatin over water and let dissolve, about 5'
3. uncover cream mixture and bring just to a simmer again over medium heat, then remove from heat
4. add gelatin and stir until dissolved; remove vanilla bean husks

5. pour into ramekins or small bowls and let cool to room temp; cover w/saran wrap and refrigerate at least 3 hours (will last up to 3 days)
6. serve with warm berries

-- had this as an amuse bouche at a fine Chicago restaurant once; brilliant --

POACHED PEARS IN RED WINE

about 20 min; serves 4

We've got pears, and we've got wine in the Gorge, and this combination is extremely good as a dessert, especially in the fall or winter months. This is a simple version of the recipe, which often calls for more spice or different liquid additions. Try it simple before branching out; this is very good.

Serve warm with some of the poaching liquid. Add whipped cream or a little ice cream if you want, but really not necessary.

Ingredients

2 C red wine

2 C water

¼ C sugar

zest from one lemon or orange

juice from the same lemon (or orange)

2 Bartlett or Bosc pears, peeled, ends cut off, cut in half and seeded

Preparation

1. add first five ingredients together in a saucepan and bring to light boil
2. reduce to simmer and add pears; simmer about 15 to 20 minutes, or until pears are tender to a fork
3. remove pears from poaching liquid and place in individual bowls
4. add some poaching liquid to each bowl and serve

5. whipped cream or a scoop of ice cream optional
6. [other options include adding cinnamon sticks or cardamom to the poaching liquid]

-- celebrate the produce of the Gorge, wherever you are! --

NORWEGIAN ALMOND COOKIES

20 min (10 active); makes ~30 cookies

This recipe (shown below) is from our mother, in her wonderful calligraphy handwriting. She didn't make these often (and I only rarely make cookies of any kind, only when there are lots of guests or visitors), but these are relatively light, and very tasty little cookies. The batter ends up very moist, so it is very hard to try to roll the batter into 'marbles' or rounds of any size, as the recipe suggests. Best bet is to use a tablespoon and try to shape some lumpy balls from the sticky batter, or put the tablespoon size lumps of batter in muffin tins instead of on a baking sheet (I use the muffin tins).

Use Saigon Cinnamon if you can find it. It's technically not cinnamon, but at the same time it's widely recognized as the most fragrant and special cinnamon available "True" cinnamon is from India/Ceylon, while Saigon cinnamon is from Southeast Asia. Both are in the genus <u>Cinnamomum</u>, but Saigon cinnamon has more essential oils, and is more closely related to <u>Cassia</u> species than other members of the cinnamon genus. Both grow as small evergreen shrubs; the inner bark is stripped and ground to make the spice. Cardomom is also from India (although also grown in Bhutan); it is one of the most expensive spices by weight, preceded by vanilla and saffron.

NORWEGIAN ALMOND COOKIES

Cream: 1 C. butter
      ½ C. sugar
      1½ t. cinnamon
      1 t. cardamom

Add and stir well:
      1 beaten egg
Add: 1⅓ C. flour
      ½ t. baking powder
      ½ C. chopped almonds

Form marbles and flatten out. Bake 10 min. at 375°

A SHORT NOTE ABOUT WINE AND THE GORGE

Wine in moderation is healthy for you, and a perfect accompaniment to good food (I Vino Veritas, you know). Nearly 50 years ago, the Pacific Northwest demonstrated that it was capable of producing some of the best wines in the world. That began with a few pioneer graduates from the University of California at Davis, starting with David Lett's Eyrie Vineyard in the Willamette Valley in the late 1960s. In 1975, an Eyrie Pinot Noir won a recognized international wine tasting competition in France, shouldering its way above famous French Burgundies.

Over the next few years, Oregon's Willamette Valley showed that it could produce excellent wines (especially Pinot Noir, due to Oregon's unique climate). Other vineyards such as Ponzi, Hillcrest, Erath and Sokol Blosser all came to prominence. Today the Willamette Valley is one of the most esteemed wine destinations in the world, with such recent superb additions as Soter, Cristom, Patricia Green, Domaine Serene, Sineann, Lange and many, many others.

More recently, the Columbia River Gorge has begun producing some very fine wines, utilizing the unique climate and terroir that exists in the Gorge. Our family established a test plot for a vineyard in Klickitat County (east of the Cascades) in the Gorge in the late 1970s, but then life took us east for a while and we had to suspend that project. We used cuttings from both Richard Lett's Eyrie vineyard and from a wonderful little Gorge start up winery that no longer exists (Mont Elise). The cuttings responded extremely well, but at the time we did not have the resources to pursue a full vineyard, and work/life took us elsewhere. But over the next few decades vineyards and wineries sprouted up all over the eastside of the Gorge. We were pleased and impressed to see our expectation of the Gorge as wine country come to life.

In 2004, the Gorge was recognized nationally by being designated with an AVA (American Viticultural Association) accreditation. The original designation included about 4,000 acres on the eastside of the Gorge, in four counties straddling the Columbia River: Hood River and Wasco counties in Oregon, and Klickitat and Skamania counties in Washington. This AVA is dramatically different than the Willamette Valley; much more dry and hot. Recently, some researchers from UC Davis have concluded that the terroir in the Columbia Gorge AVA may have the ability to produce extremely fine wines. The Columbia Gorge AVA is also almost wholly within the Columbia River Gorge National Scenic Area; all the better to visit!

The Gorge AVA contains more than 40 wineries, with many vineyards to support them. Some of our very good friends and neighbors stand out in this new effort, like Alexis and Juliet Pouillon of Domaine Pouillon winery, Don McDermott and family with the Scorched Earth vineyard, Cathedral Ridge winery and Brad Gearhart of Jacob Williams winery, and of course the Maryhill Winery. Proud of them all.

The Gorge also overlaps into a small part of the larger "Columbia Valley" AVA, which extends up through the Horse Heaven Hills to central and eastern Washington. The existing Columbia Gorge AVA may soon be split into two units, because there are some recognizable distinctions between most of the current area and a smaller area around The Dalles and similar areas across the river in Washington. Among the wonderful grapes being produced in the Columbia Gorge AVA are Syrah, Cabernet, Merlot, Zinfandel, Barbera and others.

So try some Gorge AVA wines, and visit the wineries. Better yet, add it to your menu planning!

Printed in the United States
By Bookmasters